Taking Care
of Myself2

For Teenagers and Young Adults with ASD

By Mary J. Wrobel
with contributions by Allison Rothamer

Taking Care of Myself2

All marketing and publishing rights guaranteed to and reserved by

FUTURE HORIZONS INC.

817-277-0727

817-277-2270 (fax)

E-mail: info@FHautism.com

www.FHautism.com

Cataloging in Publications Data is available from the Library of Congress.
ISBN 978-1941765302

Dedication

Special thanks to the following people for their first hand ideas, suggestions and inspiration: Cyndee Fralick, Ricky Fonseca and Lisa Mlodoch, Diane Chapman, Andrew and Hope Galloway, Sean and Susan Charles, Mary Kendzora, and Veronica Orduno and family. Your personal knowledge, ingenuity and commitment continue to inspire me to do more to support individuals with autism.

To all my students with ASD, you have continued to inspire and teach me for more than 30 years.

Acknowledgements

It's hard for me to imagine writing and producing this book without the inspiration and support of many. I am truly grateful to all those experts in the field of autism, education and health who have written and shared their knowledge in their area of expertise. I have depended on all that expert knowledge while gathering and sharing information for this book.

I am so blessed to have the support and encouragement of my family and friends. I appreciate my family for pushing me to finish this book, and believing in my ability to make a difference for the autism spectrum community. Special thanks to my "wine time" ladies. You are my cheerleaders, and you have listened to me for countless hours talk about this book, always supporting me along the way.

I couldn't have completed this book without the valuable assistance of Allison Rothamer, my daughter and writing partner. You are my second set of eyes, my personal editor and frequent sounding board.

Thanks to my husband, Tony, for his constant encouragement and sense of humor and, of course, for his expertise in "urinal etiquette."

Finally, I want to thank my many ASD students who I've taught for 30+ years. You have all inspired me in your own ways to be a better teacher and speech language pathologist. I often think of you and the lessons you have taught me.

Table of Contents

Introduction

If you are familiar with my book, Taking Care of Myself, this book could be considered a continuation, or "Part 2." This book, Taking Care of Yourself2, is different because it covers more mature topics and targets an older population, specifically older teenagers and young adults with autism, whereas my original book was written for much younger students (typically 5 to 13 year olds) with ASD.

Taking Care of Yourself2 is written for individuals on the autism spectrum to use independently, because I know that some teenagers and many adults with ASD will be able to read and understand it easily on their own. It is also written for instructors and parents to use as a means to explain difficult and sometimes sensitive life-skill topics. In each section's introduction, I include tips for instructors and parents in addition to tips for teenagers and young adults with ASD.

The six units and the topics in each section were chosen based on my experience working with students and adults with autism spectrum disorder. It also addresses the needs indicated by instructors and parents. All of the information included is knowledge that I believe teenagers and young adults with ASD would need and will use. Many of the subjects covered can be considered common knowledge, and are explained in a simple and straightforward way that I hope individuals on the spectrum will understand. And some of this information, admittedly, is my opinion, based on what I feel is important.

You will notice that certain topics I've chosen to write about may appear to be scary and alarming. Unfortunately, when dealing with topics that include personal safety, health, sex and even relationships, it's sometimes hard to explain how to solve specific problems without exposing the dangers and scarier aspects of a situation. I don't intend to cause worry or scare anyone, but I do want individuals with ASD to have a clear understanding of dangerous situations which they may face and be prepared to safely and appropriately respond to them. Nonetheless, parents may want to edit, modify or monitor some of this information, especially if you think your teen is not able to handle it quite yet.

When I instruct students with ASD about health, hygiene, puberty, personal safety, behavior, relationships and sex, I typically use visuals, Social Stories, and step-by-step instructions. For years, Mayer-Johnson has marketed an ever-growing library of line-drawn pictures to help students understand a huge range of vocabulary, including sex-related terms. Boardmaker Pictures, also known as Picture Communication Symbols (PCS), is a popular choice, if you are looking for line-drawn pictures to help illustrate any of the information presented here. Also, new picture systems keep emerging. LessonPix is another line-drawn picture system with a huge library of affordable pictures you can use. There are many options available to you, with new choices being developed almost constantly.

If you find you need photos to illustrate certain information, check out Picture This, Functional Living Skills and Behavioral Rules CD, and Picture This Professional DVD by Silver Lining Multimedia, Inc. I have also found photos on Google Images, but it may be necessary to abide by copyright laws if you copy and use photos from the Internet.

I often write Social Stories for students who need a visual approach to understand information, particularly regarding how a specific situation relates to them personally. There are no Social Stories in this book, but it should be easy enough to create Social Stories from the instructional information included in each section.

Many students work well with lists, checklists, and step-by-step instructions when learning and using new information. For that reason, I have included bulleted lists, checklists and some step-by-step instructions throughout this book.

I encourage anyone using Taking Care of Yourself2 to modify, edit, simplify or expand the information presented, depending upon what your child or student with ASD needs in order to understand and use it. Although I've developed curricula and created or modified information for students with ASD, I don't think of myself as a writer. I am more comfortable solving problems and finding ways to teach students on the autism spectrum, then actually writing about it. I've always believed it is more important to find a method to teach every student what they need to know in a way that they will truly grasp it.

Finally, I hope this book will inspire anyone reading it to research and look for more information on the topics presented here, especially if you have questions you need answered. The more we know on these topics, the better informed and prepared we will all be.

Unit 1: Hygiene and Grooming

Introduction to Hygiene and Grooming

Everyday Grooming

Deciding Whether to Shave

Looking Your Best

We Dress for Different Events

Introduction to Hygiene and Grooming

Appearances are very important when we want to make a good first impression or just blend in with a group of people. If we want to make friends, get a job, or just be accepted and respected by others, we have to look our best. That means being clean and tidy and wearing appropriate clothing in all situations.

Unfortunately, we are often judged by our appearance, and this is especially true for people with autism and other disabilities. One of the popular strategies for individuals with autism is to pretend to be like everyone else, and that starts with looking like everyone else.

When people are well dressed, their quirks are more often overlooked than if their appearance seems odd or unusual. When you look good, other people are more forgiving of confusing or inappropriate behaviors that you might exhibit. Being clean, smelling good, wearing nice clothes and accessories, and having an appealing and appropriate hairstyle all contribute to how we appeal to and impress others. When we are clean and wearing appropriate, fashionable clothing, we not only look attractive, but we also feel more confident.

Teenagers and adults need to be in the habit of daily grooming, which usually involves a daily shower and thoroughly washing your body with soap, water and shampoo, followed by applying deodorant and wearing clean underwear and clothing. Other daily grooming activities include brushing and flossing teeth, possibly using mouthwash, and handwashing frequently throughout the day, especially after using the bathroom, before eating, after touching dirty objects, or getting anything dirty and sticky on our hands. Combing and styling our hair and shaving unwanted body hair are also part of the daily grooming process. Applying body lotion, makeup and perfume/cologne are also grooming options. If you are a teenager or adult, daily grooming is a must, whether you want to make a good impression or just blend in.

Fashion and clothing accessories are often changing, and you need to update your clothes to have the appropriate attire to wear to specific events and activities. Wearing the right clothes in the right way in a variety of situations is always a challenge and can sometimes be difficult to learn.

If possible, teens and young adults with ASD and related disabilities should choose their own clothing with some guidance from peers and caregivers. Parents or caregivers, if you still need to select and purchase clothing for your post-adolescent child, be sure to pay attention to what his/her peers are wearing, even if, as an adult, he/she doesn't care for the styles and fashions of the peer group. The idea is to help your child fit in.

Be mindful of inappropriate clothing choices, such as anything too revealing, or, in some cases, gang colors and styles. Pay attention to inappropriate emblems, symbols or wording on clothing which may be offensive to others. Sometimes clothing and accessories can bring unwanted attention, invite ridicule or cause anger among others.

If you are a teenager and are part of a club, team or organization, then by all means, dress yourself to identify with those in your group/team/club, etc. By wearing the group's shirts and emblems (swim team, chess club, and jazz choir), it shows others that you are a member of and belong to a particular group. You become identified with this group, and to some extent may be protected by the members of this group. In high school, it is important to be included in one or more groups, because being a loner and unattached from a group of peers isolates you even more from others and can often invite bullying.

Teenagers and young adults with ASD and related disabilities need to understand the importance of daily grooming and choosing appropriate clothing to wear for a variety of situations. You need to learn to observe the grooming and fashion of your peers and then apply it to yourself. This is part of your journey of independence, as you develop your own style while also conforming to the social rules of your peers. In this section, we will address the importance of good hygiene, grooming and clothing, and how to look and feel your best in all situations.

Tips for Teachers/Instructors:

- Use photos or line drawings to illustrate instructional stories.
- Create grooming checklists that students can use at school or home.
- During group activities, talk about what you can wear to school and encourage student discussions about what is appropriate and popular to wear.
- Encourage students to observe their peers and make lists of what they see neuro-typical students wearing.
- Problem-solve grooming techniques and help students determine grooming priorities.
- If you notice an individual's grooming problem or suspect that a student isn't grooming properly, address this with the student first, and if necessary, contact the parent.
- Try to make grooming and dressing the responsibility of the student instead of the parent.

Tips for Parents:

- Allow your ASD teen privacy in the bathroom and bedroom and encourage your teen to wash and dress by him- or herself.
- Place grooming/washing reminders in the bedroom and bathroom for your teen, if necessary. You can work with the school to create illustrated and laminated checklists and reminders.
- Look through magazines with your teen and find peer-appropriate clothes, hairstyles, and accessories that he/she might like.
- Discuss changes with your teen that he/she might need to make to fit in better and look like other students at school.
- Make sure your teen has the washing and grooming items he/she needs in the bathroom (deodorant, shampoo, combs, body wash, razors, etc.).
- Make sure your teen is wearing clean, neat, and appropriate clothing every day. Don't let him/her wear the same clothes every day or the same outfit more than twice a week.

Tips for Teens and Young Adults with ASD:

- After puberty, you will sweat more, stink more and your body will produce more oil. As a result, it's important to shower daily and clean yourself thoroughly with soap and shampoo.
- Use deodorant/antiperspirant daily on clean underarms and wear clean underwear every day.
- Look in the mirror before you leave for school or work. Make sure you look your best and that your hair is clean and styled nicely.
- Develop your own style of dressing, but keep your clothes up-to-date with the current trends and appropriate for the occasion.
- If you don't know what to wear to an event, ask a friend or co-worker. Check with friends if you are uncertain about your apparel or hairstyle.
- For help with styling hair or applying makeup, you can ask friends for tips, look in fashion magazines and watch video tutorials on makeup and hair. YouTube offers an endless collection of tutorials for just about every makeup or hair technique.

Everyday Grooming

There are some things we need to do every day to look, feel, and smell our best.

You should shower daily with soap and water, because you can get dirty and stinky. You can shower either in the morning or in the evening. You can decide when it's best for you to shower. Some people shower every day, and some people shower every other day. Many people, especially women, do not wash their hair every day, but it is still important to wash your body every day or every other day to avoid smelling bad. If you shower without soap or shampoo, you will not get clean, and your body will probably still smell stinky, and you will have greasy hair.

Remember to clean every part of your body when you shower. You especially need to wash your face, feet, your privates and under your arms. These are the places on your body which can become more oily and stinky than the rest of you.

After your shower, when you're clean and dry, put on an antiperspirant or deodorant under your arms (in your armpits). You should only put deodorant/antiperspirant in clean armpits. If your armpits are already dirty and stinky, deodorant won't be very effective, and you might still smell bad.

You can choose to put on a body lotion if your skin feels dry. Many lotions have a pleasant scent. If you want lotion with no scent, you can usually find several unscented lotion options at a store. Many people put lotion on after a shower, because a shower can sometimes make your skin dry. Your skin might also be drier in the winter, causing you to put on more lotion than usual in the winter, especially on your hands.

You should always wear clean socks and underwear each day. Even if you wear clothes more than once before washing them, you always need to put on clean socks and underwear, because socks and underwear will get stinky and dirty every day. The armpit of a shirt might also get stinky after being worn, and once it is stinky, it should not be worn again until it is washed. After exercising or playing sports, you will probably also get sweaty and stinky. You should shower and probably should not wear those clothes again until they are cleaned. If you aren't sure whether a shirt needs to be cleaned, you can hold it up to look for stains and dirt and smell the armpits of the shirt. If the shirt smells stinky or looks dirty, don't wear it again until it has been cleaned.

Once you are clean, you shouldn't wear dirty or smelly clothing. A shower won't help you feel and smell clean if you're wearing dirty underwear and socks. Remember to change into clean underwear and socks each day after your shower.

If your hair gets especially dirty and greasy, you may need to wash it every day with shampoo. If you don't need to wash your hair every day, you should still comb or brush it to keep it looking neat and tidy. If your hair looks only a little bit greasy in some places, you can spray dry shampoo in those spots and brush it out with a brush.

You should brush your teeth with a toothbrush and toothpaste every day. Brushing your teeth and flossing between your teeth keeps your teeth clean and helps prevent cavities and gum disease. Brushing your teeth also helps to give you clean, fresh breath and keeps your teeth and gums looking nice. No one likes talking to someone with smelly, bad breath or dirty teeth. Yuck! Some people brush their teeth only once a day, and some people brush their teeth twice or more each day. People often like to brush their teeth in the morning and at night before bed. Before going anywhere, you should look at your teeth in the mirror to make sure your teeth and gums look clean and that there is no food stuck in your teeth. If your teeth need cleaning, you should clean them, no matter what time of day it is.

It is important to have clean and trimmed nails every day. You do not need to cut or clean your nails every day, but you should look at them to make sure they look clean and tidy. Men and boys often choose to have their nails cut short, but it is still important to make sure there isn't dirt under the nails and that the nails are not sharp or jagged. Women and girls may have nails that are short or nails that are long. Some women grow very long nails or get fake nails glued on at a nail salon. It is easy to take care of short nails – just make sure they are clean and tidy! If you have longer nails, you may need to clean under them, file them, and paint them more frequently. Many women with long nails or fake nails go to a nail salon regularly, because their nails need more care to look good.

We all want to look, feel and smell our best. Everyday grooming is something we all need to do routinely.

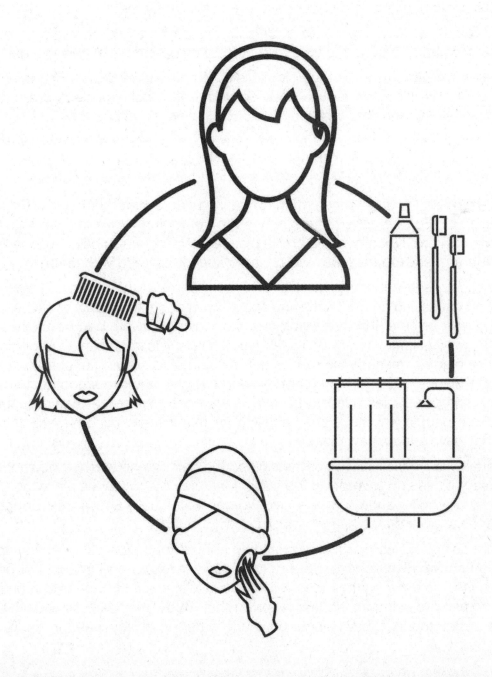

Deciding Whether to Shave

Shaving unwanted body hair is something many adults do. Most young adults begin to shave some unwanted body hair when they are teenagers. The amount and thickness of hair that grows on your body, and where it grows, are different for every person.

Men will often shave some or all of their facial hair off or any hair growing on their face and neck. Men may choose to grow facial hair, such as a beard or moustache, and may decide to only trim facial hair when it's needed. Some men even choose to shave the hair on their head. Some men will grow enough hair to make a good beard, goatee or mustache, and some won't. Men who choose to grow a beard will often still shave their upper cheeks and their neck of extra hairs, and they will regularly comb and trim their beard, mustache or goatee to keep it neat and tidy.

Men don't typically shave their leg hair or underarm hair. Usually the only men who shave body hair, including legs and underarms, are certain athletes.

Young women usually choose to start shaving leg and underarm hair when they are teenagers, which is around the time they start to grow underarm hair and darker leg hair.

If women have part or most of their legs visible to others, such as when they wear skirts, capris or shorts, it's important to have shaved legs. Unshaved legs are uncommon on women in the U.S. and may look weird to anyone who might see them.

Young women, especially those who wear sleeveless tops, shave their underarm hair. Most women think their underarm hair looks bad and it can be a big turn-off to others who might see it. Women often think shaved underarms look, feel and smell cleaner.

Teenage girls and young women might be teased and avoided if they have visible leg and underarm hair. Furthermore, people may not be attracted to women who have visible leg and underarm hair. Not all women shave their leg and underarm hair. If women don't shave their underarm and leg hair, they will typically keep it covered with clothing.

People usually shave in the privacy of their bathrooms in their homes, using a razor and some kind of shaving cream or shaving soap. If you don't know how to shave, ask an older brother, sister or parent before trying it on your own. Shaving can be tricky and cause a few cuts until you know how to do it well. If you shave, it is important to periodically change your razor blades, because the blades get dull and stop shaving effectively. Having sharp new razor blades and shaving cream or soap will give you the smoothest shave, but the new and sharper blades need to be used very gently, because they can cut skin more easily. Even people who have been shaving for many years will often still cut themselves when they have a fresh new razor.

Men usually shave their face over the sink so the hair can be washed down the sink drain or be easily picked up to throw in the trash. Men also like to have a mirror so they can see what they are doing and do a nice job. Women will usually shave their armpits and legs while in the shower so the hair is washed down the drain.

If you are using an electric razor, you should not get the razor wet or use soap and water when you shave. Electric razors are not like regular razors and should not get wet! Men using an electric razor on their face will still usually shave their face over a bathroom sink, and if women are using an electric razor on their body, they will still usually shave in the shower or bathtub, but they will not have any water on or any water in the bathtub. After they are done shaving with an electric razor, they might take a shower or rinse the trimmed hairs down the drain.

Men might shave their face hair every day, because facial hair usually grows fast. Women might shave their leg and underarm hair in the shower every day, every other day, or every two days, depending on how fast their body hair grows. Most women shave their legs and underarm hair more often in hotter months, when they are wearing less clothing. In the winter, when armpits and legs are covered by clothing and no one is going to see them, women might not shave as often.

As a young adult, shaving is a choice you will make. What or how much you shave is up to you. Remember, most teenage girls and women will keep their legs and underarms shaved on a regular basis. And even though men do not shave their legs and underarms, they will usually shave their faces of some or all hair.

Looking Your Best

You may not care how you look most of the time. You might not care that your face is dirty or your hair is uncombed. Maybe you don't care if your clothes are dirty, wrinkled or mismatched. These kinds of things might not matter to you. In fact, most people don't really care how they look when they are home alone, with no one to see them.

Looking your best is important when you're with others. Everyone wants to look their best when other people are seeing them.

When you go to school or work, you need to look your best. Also, when you go to parties or social events, you need to look your best. Looking your best means you need to be clean, and your hair and clothes are tidy and clean, too. Sometimes looking your best might mean you won't just look and smell clean, but you will also be wearing very nice clothes, with special jewelry or expensive accessories. For women, looking your best might mean having a beautiful hairstyle and nice makeup, such as lipstick, eye shadow and mascara.

There are many ways to look your best. Looking your best always starts with being clean. People don't like to be around other people who look and smell dirty. People will usually be uncomfortable and sometimes disgusted if anyone near them has not bathed in a while and if someone is wearing the same dirty clothes for more than a day.

To look your best, you especially need a clean face, hands and hair. You also need to smell nice and clean. Frequently showering with soap and water and wearing deodorant will make you smell and look nice and clean.

Your hands and nails should also be clean. No one wants to shake hands that are dirty or sticky. People also don't want to touch anything that has been touched by dirty hands. You should wash your hands several times a day, especially after you blow your nose, after using the toilet, and before you eat or touch food. It's also a good idea to wash your hands after touching something you know is dirty and full of germs.

You should always have clean and tidy-looking hair. This means you may need to wash your hair regularly and also comb or brush your hair every day. Your hair also needs to be in an appropriate haircut and hairstyle. Hairstylists can help you choose a hair style and cut that would look and work best for you.

Your clothes also need to be neat and clean and fit you well. Try to wear clothes that match or go together. People will think there is something wrong with you if your clothes are dirty, very mismatched or very wrinkled and untidy looking. You won't look your best if your clothes are too small, too big, tattered or damaged looking.

Before getting dressed, look at your clothes and plan the outfits you want to wear. Think about tops, pants, socks and shoes that go together and look good together. Don't wear anything too old, unfashionable or damaged.

When you are dressed, check yourself out in a full-length mirror. Does your outfit look good, and do the parts of your outfit go together? Does what you are wearing look fashionable? Do you look like your peers at school or work? Do you look clean, and does your hair look nice? Do you look and feel attractive and confident? These are all things you need to think about before you leave the house to start your day. If you look good and you are wearing a stylish outfit, you will feel attractive and confident.

Create your own checklist, which you can refer to before leaving your home.

My Grooming Checklist

✓ I'm wearing clean clothes, which are appropriate for the day's activities.
✓ My clothes match or go together well.
✓ My clothes aren't too old, faded or out of fashion.
✓ My clothes fit me and aren't too short, long, big or small.
✓ My clothes look nice – There are no rips, holes, stains, missing buttons or broken zippers.
✓ My clothes look tidy and are not too wrinkled.
✓ My shoes, socks, belt and other accessories go with my outfit.
✓ My shoes and coat are clean.
✓ My hair is clean and combed and styled nicely.
✓ My teeth are clean and my breath is fresh.
✓ My nails are clean and do not have dirt underneath.
✓ My face and hands are clean.
✓ I look good!

We Dress for Different Events

Everyone wears clothing every day. There are rules to wearing clothes, including what to wear for specific events and situations. Most people have a sense of what they should wear when they attend events and activities as well as what they should wear to school or work.

If you want to fit in with your peers and wear appropriate clothes when you are attending different events, you need to follow some clothing rules.

Your clothes should always fit you. Your clothes shouldn't be too small or too big. Besides being clean, your clothes need to be in good condition. It is okay to wear ripped, stained and faded clothes at home, but if you're at work or school, you should make sure your clothes look nice and are fashionable. It's often fashionable to wear ripped or faded jeans, but only for casual occasions, such as going to school or for hanging out with friends. Be sure your style of clothing is appropriate for where you are going.

You should routinely check your clothes for holes, missing buttons, broken zippers and stains. It's usually not appropriate to wear worn-out and damaged clothing to work and possibly not to school. If you are going to a nice party or a formal event such as a wedding, funeral or a dance, you may need to wear more dressy-looking clothing.

You would typically wear tidy, nicer clothes to work, but wear casual, more comfortable clothes when you're at a sports event or hanging out with your friends. Sometimes if you go to a formal party or special event, you may need to get dressed up in your best clothes. Men may be required to wear a suit and tie to a formal event, such as a wedding. Likewise, women usually need to wear a nice dress to a wedding. If you don't know what to wear, you can always ask others who are also attending the event what you should wear. Women often ask other women what they are wearing to an event to help themselves decide what they will wear.

Your shoes should be clean and in good condition. Like clothing, you need to wear shoes that are appropriate for where you are going and what you are doing. We typically wear fancy, dressy shoes with fancy and formal clothing. We wear comfortable, work-appropriate shoes to work, and we usually wear casual, sporty shoes or sandals to school or for just hanging out with friends.

There are times when people should not wear nice clothes. Usually when you are painting, working in a yard, building something, or cleaning a dirty place like a garage, we will choose to wear clothes that are old and damaged. We don't usually care if our old, damaged clothing gets more damaged, dirty or full of paint.

If you're not sure what to wear or how your hair should look, you can look at others your age to see what they are wearing and doing. What kinds of clothes and shoes are people your age wearing? What are some nice hairstyles for people your age? You can also look in magazines to get clothing and hairstyle ideas. You can even ask those who work or live with you to help you look your best.

Every day before you leave home for work, school or somewhere else, you should check your appearance in the mirror. Do you look clean and tidy? Do your clothes match and look nice? Do you look your best? How do you look compared to your peers or co-workers?

You can wear whatever you want at home, but it's important to look your best when you're with others. You need to remember to always be clean and look neat and tidy when you are with other people, no matter what you're doing.

Some Fashion Rules for When You Are Around Other People:

1. Always wear clean clothes that fit you appropriately.
2. Your clothes and shoes should match or go together well.
3. Your clothing shouldn't be too wrinkled, too faded or messy looking.
4. Your clothing shouldn't be too worn-out or damaged, unless you are painting, cleaning or building and don't want to wear your good clothes.
5. Make sure your clothes and shoes aren't too old or totally out of fashion with the clothes your peers are wearing.
6. Make sure your clothing is appropriate for where you are going, such as work, a date, a sports event or a wedding.
7. Be sure to have a variety of clothing items and shoes for everyday activities, such as work and school.
8. Don't wear the same clothes every day, even if they are clean.
9. Don't wear the same pair of shoes every day and to every event.
10. Try to wear individual shirts and dresses only once a week.
11. Check yourself out in a mirror before you leave home to be sure you look clean, tidy and ready to go.

Your peers will more likely approach you and enjoy being near you when you are wearing clean, attractive, and appropriate-looking clothing. When you are dressed similarly as your peers, it helps you fit in with them, and it tells your peers that you can look and be like them.

Unit 2: Staying Healthy

Introduction to Staying Healthy

Getting and Staying Healthy

Eating Right

Taking Care of Your Teeth and Mouth

Dealing with Sickness

Dealing with Pain

Check Your Body for Changes

DEPRESSION

When Should You See a Doctor?

Dealing with Allergies

Feeling Anxious

Dealing with Depression

Drug and/or Alcohol Abuse and Addiction

If You Feel Suicidal

Staying in a Hospital

Introduction to Staying Healthy

Learning to be responsible for your own body and health is a big step toward independence, and it's an important one. As individuals enter adolescence and adulthood, modesty and self-care become a priority. Parents and caregivers should be doing less and less for young ASD adults as they learn to do more for themselves. As these young adults become more independent, perhaps even living on their own, it's vitally important that they pay attention to changes in their bodies and health and learn to take care of themselves to the best of their ability.

Demonstrating modesty typically means bathing and dressing independently, and usually alone. This also means that, if a child is dressing and bathing alone, parents and guardians are no longer observing health changes first hand. Parents would typically notice potential health problems, such as infections, sores, unusual moles, lumps and discoloring on their child's body when bathing or dressing. When parents no longer have a hand in bathing and dressing, it becomes the responsibility of the adolescent or young adult to notice any health and body changes and know how to handle any potential problems.

Parents would usually be able to tell if their child is sick, acting unusual or out-of-sorts. Parents can usually determine minor health problems versus more serious problems as well as how to handle them. As children get older and become young adults, it's vital that they learn about being healthy and make certain health determinations on their own.

Talking to students and children about health problems can be risky. Some individuals with autism may become terrified about the possibility of contracting various health conditions and diseases. It's important that they understand health problems and use that information to problem-solve and determine what to do when something arises. It's also important to explain the specifics of health problems in a calm, matter-of-fact manner and to reassure your children or students of the little likelihood of it happening to them, especially if they know how to be healthy and responsible and act on any potential health problems, if they occur.

We cannot ignore the prevalence of anxiety and depression in the ASD population. Autism has a strong link to anxiety and depression, and most individuals with ASD, including children, deal with varying degrees of anxiety and depression in their day-to-day lives. The following information further emphasizes the need to address anxiety and depression in adolescents and young adults with ASD.

We know that anxiety can lead to depression and "anxiety is inherent in ASD" (Nick Dubin).

Children with autism who experience anxiety will very likely develop depression as adolescents and adults. Fifty percent of higher-functioning ASD adolescents contemplate suicide. They are at a fifty percent higher risk of suicide than neuro-typical adolescents (Greg Siegle). Many adults with autism have bouts of depression and are five times more likely to attempt suicide than adults without autism (Sarah DeWeerdt, 2014).

The way individuals with ASD think makes them more vulnerable to depression and suicide. It doesn't occur to them that they need help and can get help. Isolation, social rejection and poor communication also put them at greater risk (Tony Attwood).

We need to be hyper-vigilant about recognizing anxiety and depression with individuals with ASD. Also, because of their autism, their symptoms of depression may present differently from those of neuro-typical individuals.

The risk of addiction among the ASD population is becoming significant, due to the fact that many ASD individuals will experience depression, anxiety or often both. It was originally thought that individuals with ASD would generally not abuse drugs or alcohol, but that belief is changing. Most studies regarding individuals on the autism spectrum and addiction are new, but more statistics are emerging. So far, studies are now showing that teens and adults with ASD, especially higher functioning individuals, are often likely to abuse and become addicted to alcohol or drugs.

The following health information is written in a way that many adolescents and adults with autism will understand and be able to follow through on the necessary information and instruction. Much of the information presented in this section is typical health information which most people are aware of, such as ways to get and stay healthy, what to do when you are sick or injured, and daily health routines. The exception to this is the information about anxiety, depression and suicide.

Tips for Teachers/Instructors:

- Pay attention to ASD students' mental and emotional health. Assume that there is inherent anxiety and possible depression. Provide small group therapy sessions to discuss and problem-solve bouts of anxiety, depression, and other health issues.
- Modify or provide an appropriate health curriculum for students with ASD and other disabilities to meet their specific needs.
- Educate ASD students and other students with disabilities about substance abuse.
- Provide people who are qualified to help ASD students who are dealing with severe anxiety, depression, and suicidal thoughts.

Tips for Parents:

- Emphasize good health practices at home.
- Make sure your son/daughter takes any medications properly and responsibly.
- Discuss health problems and emergencies as they come up. Help your child feel assured and confident instead of scared or concerned.
- Assume your child has anxiety and possibly depression; address those issues, including talking and working with doctors to find appropriate meds and therapy.
- Emphasize the safe use of prescribed medication, and monitor any medication your teen or young adult is taking.
- Look for warning signs that may indicate that your son or daughter is thinking about suicide, and if he/she ever mentions suicide or ending his/her life, take it very seriously. Listen to what he/she says about his/her feelings and get help immediately!

Tips for Teens and Young Adults with ASD:

- Pay attention to your health and create healthful routines which are best for you.
- Pay attention to your body, and if you suspect a health problem or condition, calmly contact a parent or trusted adult and possibly your doctor.
- If you have a life-threatening condition and you know you need help immediately, call 911.
- Be sure to take any medicine prescribed to you according the instructions from the doctor and on the medicine bottle. Do not self-medicate with other meds not prescribed by your doctor.
- Stay away from substances that are dangerous to your health, such as tobacco products, alcohol, and illegal drugs.
- If you are unable to manage your anxiety and/or you have symptoms of severe depression, contact your doctor.
- If you have suicidal thoughts, call 911, tell a trusted adult or contact your doctor immediately!

Getting and Staying Healthy

Being healthy means taking care of your body and doing all that you can to stay well, strong, and feeling your best.

It's important for you to take good care of your body so that you don't get sick or hurt. You only have one body, and you need to take care of it every day.

You need to eat healthy foods, which are good for your body and drink plenty of water to stay well hydrated all day. Eating healthy consists of having a balanced diet of fruits, vegetables, grains and protein, such as lean meats, fish, beans and nuts. It also includes eating healthy fats and oils, such as olive oil and unsaturated fats.

Taking care of your teeth is something you should do every day to stay healthy. Ideally, you should brush your teeth twice a day and floss once a day. Some people even rinse their mouths out with mouthwash to kill bacteria and germs in their mouths. Brushing and flossing your teeth every day will keep your teeth and gums healthy.

Take a bath or shower every day with soap and warm water. You need to clean your whole body to remove dirt, germs and smelly odors. You need to wash your hair with shampoo when it gets dirty and greasy, and rinse out the shampoo with clean, warm water.

You need to get plenty of sleep every night. You will probably need to get seven to nine hours of good, dream-filled sleep each night. Sleeping will rest your brain and help you think better. Sleeping also keeps your body healthy. If you don't get enough sleep, you will have a hard time concentrating, and you might get sick more easily.

You need to stay hydrated by drinking lots of clean water every day. If you don't drink enough water, you could become dehydrated and sick. Besides feeling thirsty, being dehydrated could make you feel weak and faint. Your body needs water every day to stay healthy. If your urine is a very dark yellow instead of a pale yellow, you probably aren't drinking enough water.

You need to wash your hands several times a day – before you eat, after you use the toilet, and whenever you blow or clean your nose. Your hands touch many dirty, germ-covered things during the day. Washing your hands frequently each day will keep germs off your hands and keep you from getting sick.

You should try and get some exercise every day. Exercise is good for your whole body and mind. Exercise will help you feel good and keep your body strong. You can choose to walk or run for about 20 minutes a day. You can ride a bike, or play a sport, like basketball or tennis. You can do exercises at home or in a gym. People who like to swim can exercise by swimming in a pool. There are lots of ways to exercise, and you should find ways to exercise your body that you enjoy.

If you get sick or have pain from an injury, you need to take care of yourself. That usually means you need to get plenty of rest and drink enough fluids if you're sick. This also means "taking it easy" or taking care of any injury, if you've hurt yourself. It's important that you tell a parent or trusted adult whenever you get sick or injured. If necessary, you may need to see a doctor if you're too sick or injured to take care of yourself.

When you get anxious and upset, you need to calm yourself down. Find ways to be calm and happy. You should also have good friends who make you laugh and feel happy. When you feel calm and happy, you will feel good about yourself. If you become anxious and sad all the time and your attempts to calm yourself down don't work, get help from your parents and your doctor.

It's important to avoid substances which can be dangerous and will harm your body. Tobacco products such as cigarettes, cigars, and chewing tobacco can cause cancer and other diseases. Smoking cigarettes or using any other tobacco products (including e-cigarettes and vaping devices) can become addictive, and it may be hard to stop once you start using them.

Drinking alcoholic beverages such as beer, wine, vodka, and whiskey can be dangerous, especially if you drink too much. Alcohol can also become addictive, and drinking too much alcohol will impair your judgment and can cause you to be sick, vomit or pass out. By law, only adults who are 21 and older can buy alcoholic drinks in the U.S. It is illegal to buy alcohol for people who are under the age of 21.

Illegal drugs such as cocaine, heroin, and methamphetamines are very dangerous. These drugs are not only very addictive, but they can also cause you to die if you take them. You should never take illegal drugs, and you should never try any drug or pill that someone gives you, especially if it's a pill you're not suppose to take. Only take over-the-counter medication such as aspirin or acetaminophen and the medicines that your doctor prescribes for you, and be sure to follow the directions on the pill bottle carefully.

Taking care of your body and your health means remembering to do many things to keep your body safe and healthy. You need to eat well, drink water, get plenty of sleep, and clean yourself every day. Get regular exercise, and take care of yourself if you get sick or injured. See your doctor and dentist at least once a year for check-ups. Be careful to stay away from things such as tobacco, alcohol, and dangerous drugs that may cause your body and mind harm.

You only have one body, and it's your responsibility to take good care of it and stay healthy.

Eating Right

There are many books, magazine articles and websites about how to eat right. Most doctors and diet experts will agree that a healthy diet is a balanced diet. A balanced diet is usually one with appropriate portions of carbohydrates and plenty of vegetables, fruits, protein and fats. A good, balanced diet is not only important to help us stay healthy, but it is also important to avoid developing health problems such as heart disease, cancer, diabetes and obesity.

Most health experts will tell us to eat plenty of vegetables, beans, seeds and nuts, fruits and whole grains. We also need to eat good fats, such as olive oil, coconut oil and other unsaturated oils. Dairy foods, such as eggs, milk, cheese and yogurt are good sources of calcium and protein and are typically good for us. Chicken, turkey, fish and tofu are good lean sources of protein, and many experts advise that red meat should be eaten in smaller portions and usually not as often.

As we get older, we need to be careful not to get too overweight. When your body is overweight, it may cause you to have bad health and lead to possible diseases. When people become adults or if they become overweight, they need to think about cholesterol levels, sugar levels, and their heart health. That's why it's important to have good, healthy eating habits. Your doctor will tell you what foods you need to eat and which foods to limit or avoid in your diet.

It is recommended that we avoid eating too much sugar, including sugary drinks and sodas. We need to limit processed foods and foods that are fried in or contain saturated fats. We should avoid eating any trans fats, as they are very unhealthy for us. Trans fats (hydrogenated or partially-hydrogenated fats and oils) are often found in boxes of cookies, snack cakes, candies, and bags of chips and other snacks. We don't want to eat very much of those junk foods, because trans fats are not good for us at all.

Almost everybody loves snacks, desserts, pizza and fast food, but too much of those foods is usually bad for us. You can treat yourself to those foods occasionally, but you probably shouldn't eat them every day.

Eating a healthy, balanced diet, whether you want to lose weight or just stay healthy, is one of the surest ways to feel your best. To eat right, you should eat most or all the foods in a balanced diet. In other words, you should consume lots of vegetables and fruits, some whole-grain breads and pastas, protein (dairy, nuts, meats, beans), and good saturated fats.

If you only eat one kind of food (for example, only eating breads and pasta), you won't necessarily get enough of the right nutrients that you need to be healthy. If you only eat junk food, such as chips, candy and French fries, you will be unhealthy, and you won't be getting the nutrients your body needs.

If you know you are allergic to certain foods, or just can't eat certain foods, be sure to find appropriate food substitutes for the specific foods you can't eat. If you are a vegetarian or if you cannot have dairy, be sure you eat enough good sources of plant-based protein, such as nuts, seeds, beans and tofu. If you cannot have wheat gluten, instead of grains, you can have corn, rice and gluten-free breads and pastas.

Staying appropriately hydrated is also very important. Most health experts will advise you to drink 4-8 glasses of clean water each day, depending on your activity level, to stay sufficiently hydrated. If you don't drink enough water each day, you may feel very sick or tired.

Many adults occasionally drink alcoholic beverages. This is a choice adults can make. A person age 21 or over in the U.S. can legally choose to purchase and drink an alcoholic beverage. An occasional glass of wine or beer is often considered good for your health. However, drinking too much alcohol, whether it's wine, beer, liqueur, whiskey or other alcoholic spirits, can be very damaging to your health and could even lead to alcoholism, which is a serious health condition and addiction. If you are concerned about drinking alcohol, or if you think you are drinking too much, consult your doctor.

Eating healthy is good for everybody. We need to eat a variety of healthy foods, drink clean water every day and limit or avoid foods or beverages that are bad for us.

Taking Care of Your Teeth and Mouth

Brushing and flossing your teeth need to be done 1 to 3 times a day as a part of your daily grooming routine. Cleaning and taking care of your teeth and mouth are important for your health.

Bacteria enters your mouth every day. Daily brushing and flossing of your teeth remove bacteria and germs from your mouth and keep your teeth and gums healthy. You can also choose to use mouthwash to kill germs and bacteria in your mouth. Mouthwash will typically give you fresh, minty breath.

You should to go to the dentist at least once a year. The dentist will check your mouth for cavities and other problems, and the dental hygienist will give your teeth a thorough cleaning. The dentist and dental hygienist will work with you to keep your teeth and gums healthy. If they notice a problem, such as a cavity or infection, they will take care of it. It's also important to call your dentist if you have a toothache or if you notice a sore or infection in your mouth.

Some people don't like going to the dentist. If you don't see your dentist when you're supposed to, you can develop lots of painful and unhealthy problems with your teeth and mouth.

Refusing to go to the dentist could cause you to develop some unpleasant and unhealthy problems in your mouth.

TEETH CLEANING

10 Reasons to See Your Dentist (Angela Ayles, ActiveBeat.com)

1.   Tooth pain – This can arise due to cavities or a tooth infection.
2.   Inflamed and painful gums – These can occur due to tooth plaque or infection.
3.   White spots on your teeth – This is often the first sign that your teeth enamel might be dissolving.
4.   Sensitivity to hot and cold in your mouth – This is often a sign of tooth decay/cavities in your teeth.
5.   Changes of color or lumps in your mouth – This may be a sign of a disease or infection.
6.   Canker or cold sores, especially frequent canker sores or sores that don't go away – This may be a sign of disease.
7.   Dry mouth – This may be a sign of bacteria or disease in your mouth.
8.   Headaches – Headaches and achy jaw may be due to grinding teeth at night.
9.   Bad breath – If you have very bad breath most of the time, you may have gingivitis.
10.   Metallic taste in your mouth – This may be a sign of gingivitis or periodontitis.

You know that your dentist is the most important person to meet with to help keep your mouth and teeth healthy. See your dentist at least once a year, and make an appointment with your dentist whenever you notice any problems in your mouth or with your teeth.

Dealing with Sickness

Everyone gets sick occasionally. Most of the time when you are sick, you could have symptoms such as a cough, stuffy nose, sore throat, headache, or an all-over achy, tired feeling. Sometimes you might feel sick to your stomach and feel like you need to throw up. These are typical sickness symptoms that you get when you have a cold or the flu. Fortunately, these typical sickness symptoms usually don't last long and shouldn't worry us too much.

Almost everyone gets a cold or the flu at least once a year. When you get sick, you might take over-the-counter pain medications like Tylenol or aspirin to reduce your pain or fever. We might take a cold medicine or something to settle your stomach. When you get sick, you usually need to drink water and other fluids and get plenty of rest until your cold or flu goes away, usually in about one week. We don't usually need to get medicine from a doctor for a cold or flu, but instead you can buy non-prescription medicine at a store and read the directions carefully before taking it.

Most sickness will eventually go away on its own as long as you get enough rest and stay hydrated with water. The non-prescription medicine you might take should decrease or eliminate your sickness symptoms until the cold or flu has run its course and you feel better.

Usually you don't even contact your doctor when you get sick with a cold or flu. If you have been sick with a cold or flu for more than two weeks and you aren't getting better, then it might be time to contact a doctor. Sometimes you need to call your doctor even after a few days or a week of being sick, especially if you get much sicker and can't control the symptoms with non-prescription medicines.

Sometimes a simple cold can become an upper respiratory infection or pneumonia. Sometimes a sore throat is caused by strep, and it gets worse if you don't get medicine to treat it. Sometimes the flu can become much worse, and you have to go to the hospital in order to get better. Anytime you get sick, you need to pay attention to what is going on with your body, and if your symptoms get worse, you need to call the doctor.

Sometimes you might feel sick and have no idea why you feel bad or sick. When you know you are sick or something is wrong, and if you are worried because you aren't getting better, then it's always a good idea to call the doctor.

It's never fun getting sick, so you need to do what you can to get better, usually by getting plenty of rest and drinking lots of water and other liquids. If you don't take care of yourself when you are sick, you could get sicker, and that is never a good thing.

There are many reasons for contacting your doctor. Sometimes you might feel sick and just know something is wrong or unusual. It's a good idea to call a parent or trusted adult if you think you may need a doctor. Trusted adults and family members can help you decide what needs to be done.

Doctors sometimes prescribe medicine for sickness. You need to follow the directions for any medicine you take, and if you have a problem or any questions about your medicine, you can call your doctor. You should never decide to stop taking your medicine or take it more or less often, unless your doctor tells you it's okay.

Dealing with Pain

Like being occasionally sick, everyone feels pain sometimes. Pain is your body's way of telling you that something is wrong, irritated or hurt. Usually the pain you feel happens because of muscle aches (when you work your muscles hard) or occasional cuts, bumps and bruises. You might get an occasional headache or a tummy ache, which goes away with a normal dose of non-prescription medicine. Most minor aches and pains go away after a short time, and you feel better.

Everyone feels some minor pain occasionally, and you can usually figure out why you have some pain, maybe from a bruise, a bumped head, a stubbed toe or a small cut. Minor, occasional pain is typically not a problem, and it usually stops quickly, even without non-prescription pain medicine. When you know what caused your pain and it is minor or goes away quickly, you don't usually need to worry about it.

Sometime you might have sharp pain in your head, called "brain freeze," when you eat something very cold quickly, like ice cream. That's a very common pain that goes away quickly, and you don't need to worry about it.

But if you have pain that doesn't go away and stay away, even with non-prescription pain medicine, it could be a more serious problem. Some pains are sharp and stabbing, while other pains might feel more dull and achy. No matter how your pain feels, it can be a problem if it doesn't go away.

You need to pay attention to any pain, and try to decide why you have it. If the pain has no explanation and it doesn't go away, you may need to check with a doctor. Do not ignore any severe pain! Any time you have sudden severe pain, especially if you have fallen or been hit by something, you should call your doctor immediately. In the case of a medical emergency, the doctor may tell you to go to an immediate care clinic or the emergency room of a hospital. A doctor will decide if your pain is serious or not.

If you have a toothache that hurts a lot and doesn't get better, you will need to see your dentist. A dentist will decide what needs to be done if you have a toothache or sore gums in your mouth.

Doctors sometimes prescribe medicine for pain. You need to follow the directions for any medicine you take, and if you have a problem or have any questions about your medicine, you should call your doctor. You should never decide to stop taking your medicine or take it more or less often unless your doctor tells you it's okay.

Check Your Body for Changes

As you get older and are bathing and dressing by yourself, hopefully in the privacy of your bedroom or bathroom, you may be the only one who will see yourself naked. Becoming independent in your self-care as you get older and becoming more modest is important. This means you need to pay attention to any changes, especially unusual ones, in your body.

Some changes, like gaining or losing weight, pimples on your face and even muscle development, are things you might notice when you look in the mirror or step on the scale. You might notice things like longer toenails and fingernails, which you need to trim. You might see hair growth, which you can decide to shave or cut. You might even notice dirty areas, which you need to do a better job cleaning. These are typical changes you will notice on your body that you can take care of yourself.

You may notice occasional pimples, rashes, small cuts or bruises. Most of the time the things you notice are not big problems, and you can usually figure out why you have those small problems or are seeing these changes. You should be able to take care of those small problems with special lotions, antiseptics or a bandage. Soon those little cuts, rashes or bruises will be gone.

Some changes can mean there's a problem that might not go away and that we can't take care of ourselves. Pay attention to changes which may tell you that something is wrong. You need to check your body occasionally, and look for anything unusual or different, especially if something you see doesn't go away or gets worse.

The following conditions may be serious and require seeing a doctor. Call your doctor if you notice any of the following conditions on your skin and body:

> **A mole that changes color, from light to dark, or becomes larger or infected – this could be an infection or a sign of skin cancer;**

> **An itchy or painful rash which becomes worse or won't go away after a few days – this may be caused by an allergy to something or could be a sign of disease;**

> **A cut which is healing very slowly or doesn't seem to be getting any better, even after a week, could be a sign of disease;**

> **A painful bump which gets bigger or redder and feels hot may be an infection;**

> **A bite or sting from an insect which gets bigger and more painful or causes you to feel sick and feverish;**

> **A lump or hard bump in or on breasts or testicles or anywhere on your body – this may be a tumor;**

> **A severe sunburn or any severe burn to your skin;**

> **A red streak that travels up your arm or leg under your skin – this may be blood poisoning and a sign of bacterial infection; Call a doctor immediately!**

> **A piece of metal, wood, insect or other material lodged in your skin that you can't get out.**

- A painful toe from an ingrown toenail, cut or infection.
- Fingernails or cuticles which change color for no particular reason –yellow, or red – this could be a sign of disease.
- Skin on your feet and toes which are rough, scaly or itchy – this may be a sign of foot fungus.
- Any unusual or unexplained changes to the color of your skin: yellowish skin, very pale skin, or more freckles on your skin – this could be a sign of disease.
- Toes or fingers that turn black or grayish white from frostbite or other damage.
- Changes to eye color which don't go away: yellowish whites of the eyes, blood-shot eyes, white rings around your iris and red and itchy eyes all could be a sign of disease or pinkeye infection.
- Cold sores on your mouth and lips – this is usually a sign of type-1 herpes or a sign of disease.
- Any painful, discolored or disfigured area on your body which doesn't get better.
- Any pus that is white, yellow or green, oozing from your skin or eyes usually indicates an infection – whenever there's an infection which doesn't start to get better after it's washed with antiseptic soap, you need to call a doctor and have it treated.
- Anything strange and unusual on your body that doesn't go away or perhaps gets worse.

We all need to pay attention to changes we see on our bodies. Little cuts and bruises happen all the time, and most of them will go away in time with careful washing, antiseptic lotions and sometimes a bandage. If you notice something which doesn't go away, changes or gets worse, then you should make an appointment with your doctor.

We are responsible for our bodies, and we need to take care of ourselves to stay healthy. Being responsible for our own bodies means taking care of problems before they get worse. We should never ignore a serious problem and just hope it goes away. We should never be afraid to go to the doctor if we think there is a problem with something on our body.

When Should You See a Doctor?

There are many reasons to see a doctor. Most people go once a year to see their doctor for a check-up or a physical exam. Some people need to have their cholesterol checked, their blood levels checked, or something else checked on a regular basis. If you have a medical condition or disease that the doctor needs to check and/or you need prescription medication, you will need to see your doctor on a routine basis.

Doctors want to be sure you are as healthy as you can be. They check you to see if there are any changes to your health or if anything is wrong or needs attention in your body.

Not everyone likes to see a doctor. Some people can be afraid of what the doctor will find or do to them. You might be afraid of shots and other procedures that a doctor might need to do, but a doctor doesn't want to hurt you. The doctor only wants to check to be sure you are healthy or will give you something, like a shot, to keep you healthy.

If you have a serious illness or suspect that something is seriously wrong with you, then you need to call your doctor for an appointment. If you call the doctor and the doctor decides you are very sick or something is seriously wrong, he/she may tell you to go to an emergency room or an immediate care clinic.

It's important to follow the doctor's orders if you have a serious medical condition that needs immediate care.

A doctor will probably want to see you if you have serious illness symptoms and are sick with something other than a cold or a mild flu.

Some symptoms of a serious illness include:

- A high fever (102 degrees and higher) or a fever that gets worse instead of better over time.
- A low-grade fever (99-101 degrees) that lasts a week or longer.
- A sore throat that doesn't feel better in three to four days, but gets worse.
- A persistent cough or hoarseness that doesn't go away after three weeks.
- Vomiting up everything you eat and drink for more than two days. If you vomit up all liquids, you can become dehydrated (not enough water in your body), and that is dangerous!
- Severe diarrhea that lasts more than a day. Remember to drink lots of water when you have diarrhea to prevent severe dehydration.
- Blood in your urine or feces.
- A constant severe headache that lasts longer than two days, and no headache medication is helping it. If you have never experienced this kind of headache before, you may want to call a doctor sooner.
- A severe rash, especially one you haven't had before.
- Difficulty breathing – Any time you have difficulty breathing for more than just a few seconds, and especially if it's happening repeatedly, call the doctor immediately!
- Chest pain or severe unexplained pain anywhere in your body.

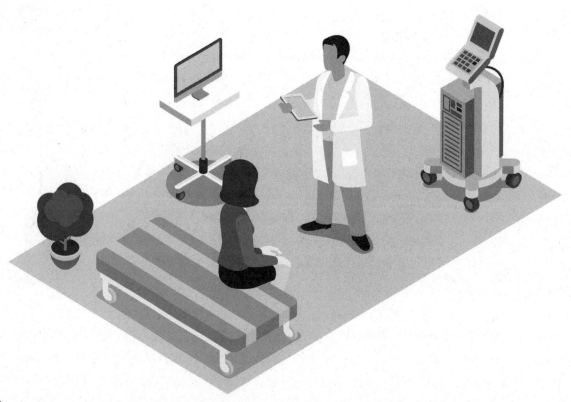

Any time there is an unexplained change to your health and especially if you have a feeling that something is wrong, you should call your doctor to see if you should be concerned. Conditions which might seem unimportant might actually be symptoms of a serious illness.

Symptoms of a serious illness might also include:

> Drastic weight loss without trying to lose weight
> Being thirsty all the time and needing to drink lots of water
> A very rapid resting heart rate when you are just sitting or lying down
> Feeling tired all the time, even when you get enough sleep
> Constant achy joints, such as knees, shoulders, feet and hands
> Frequently feeling faint or dizzy
> Weakness in arms and legs
> Unexplained muscle aches and pains
> Feeling very anxious most of the time
> Feeling very sad and depressed
> Feeling suicidal or having thoughts of suicide

There are many reasons for contacting a doctor. Sometimes you might feel sick and just know something is wrong or unusual. It's a good idea to call a parent or trusted adult if you think you might need a doctor. Trusted adults and family members can help you decide what needs to be done.

Doctors sometimes prescribe medicine for sickness. It's important to follow the directions for any medicine you take, and if you have a problem or any questions about your medicine, you should call your doctor. You should never decide to stop taking your medicine or take it more or less often unless your doctor tells you it is okay.

Dealing with Allergies

An allergy happens when your body has a strong reaction to something around you or in the environment. Your body may act as if something ordinary, like dust, is very dangerous. If that happens, you might have an allergic reaction. Having an allergic reaction means you might get a rash or hives, have difficulty breathing or feel itchy all over. Your eyes might look red and itchy. You could also have a runny nose, feel congested or have swelling in places on your body.

Many people have allergies, and you can develop an allergy at any age. Most people are allergic to things like dust, pollen, pet fur and dander, mold, and certain plants and foods. Some people are allergic to specific drugs or medicines. You can have an allergy to just one thing or be allergic to a few or more things. You can have allergies to many things.

Allergies are not comfortable, and sometimes they might make you feel miserable and sick. Most allergies are at least annoying, but some allergies can be dangerous and even life threatening. If you have an allergy, you need to pay attention to your symptoms and avoid things that will cause an allergic reaction.

If you think you have one or more allergies, you should probably talk to a doctor. A doctor can perform tests to determine specifically what you might be allergic to. A doctor can also decide how you should handle an allergy. Some allergies might need prescription medicine, but most of the time people use non-prescription medicine to manage allergy symptoms.

If you know you have a severe allergy to something that could be life threatening, be very careful to avoid whatever causes that strong or dangerous allergic reaction. You may need to tell friends, family members and co-workers about your dangerous allergy so that they can help you avoid those potentially dangerous substances. Telling others about your allergies will also help them to help you when, and if, you have a strong allergic reaction.

Having an allergy to something can be annoying and possibly dangerous. If you know as much as you can about your allergies, you can usually manage them. Many people have allergies and learn to avoid those things they are allergic to.

Avoiding situations or things that cause allergic reactions, knowing what to do if you have an allergic reaction and taking allergy medicine to prevent those reactions are all ways to keep you safe and healthy, even though you have allergies.

Feeling Anxious

Anxiety or feeling anxious happens when you have scary thoughts that worry you or make you feel afraid. When a person feels anxious, he or she may feel upset and scared because he/she thinks something bad will happen.

A person can feel anxious about many things. You might feel anxious about situations that you know can be bad or scary. Maybe you feel anxious because you had a bad experience before or you think a new situation will be bad.

People might feel anxious about going to the dentist, taking a test, making an important decision or doing something difficult or maybe dangerous. There are many reasons for feeling anxious about something.

Everyone feels anxious and upset sometimes, this is normal. Usually the anxious feelings will go away after the scary situation is finished. Most of the time, you will realize that the anxious situation was not so bad, and once it's over, you will feel better and even proud that you did a good job handling the scary, anxious situation. When the anxious situation is over, you feel good again, and feelings of anxiety go away.

If the anxious feelings don't go away and you continue to think about scary things and worry most of the time, it can be a problem. If you feel worried and fearful almost all of the time, it will affect everything you do.

Feelings of anxiety might make you feel scared and upset. It might make you do things over and over, or not let you do things you know you should do. Being very anxious might make you feel sick or make you want to run away or hurt yourself or others. Being very anxious or feeling anxious most of the time can be a big problem and even dangerous. Being too anxious is bad for you.

How do you know if you are experiencing anxiety? Anxiety can be different for everyone. Most people who experience anxiety will have some or most of these symptoms:

- Feelings of fear, uneasiness and panic just from thinking about a situation;
- Thinking about scary situations a lot;
- Having the same bad thoughts and worries over and over again;
- Having a hard time falling asleep and staying asleep;
- Having many nightmares or nightmares every night;
- Having a hard time completing tasks because of scary and worried thoughts;
- Doing things over and over again because of worried thoughts;
- Not being able to feel calm no matter what you do;
- Feeling panicky and having a hard time breathing or your heart beating too fast because of scary thoughts;
- Feeling sick to your stomach or dizzy when you have scary thoughts;
- Feeling sick or uncomfortable in other ways when you have scary thoughts.

Everyone feels anxious sometimes. Besides taking medicine, there are several ways people can prevent an anxiety attack or manage their anxious feelings.

- Tell a trusted friend, adult or family member that you think you are having an anxiety attack. Let them help you leave a situation or calm down.
- Calm yourself down with deep breathing while counting silently to 20.
- Take a break and leave the room or find a place where you can be alone for a while.
- Take a walk, exercise or dance.
- Listen to your favorite or relaxing music. If you are with others, use ear buds with an iPod.
- Meditate – close your eyes and think of nothing. Think of a relaxing mantra you can silently repeat to yourself.
- Close your eyes and picture a favorite or happy, relaxing place.
- If at home or in a work space, do an activity that relaxes you and gets your mind off any anxious thoughts.
- Do a puzzle, play a game or do any fun and relaxing activity that you enjoy doing.
- Watch a funny movie – something that will get you laughing and smiling.
- If you are alone, call a friend or family member. Sometimes just talking to a close friend or family member will help ease your anxiety.

If you worry about getting anxiety attacks or think you may get anxious when you are attending an event or when you are at school or work, try to find ways to get ahead of your anxiety and hopefully prevent anxious thoughts.

> ➢ **Make a list of what you need to do and what you need to take with you.**
> ➢ **Prepare and organize your materials, clothing and any items you will need.**
> ➢ **Map out what you expect will happen and how you will react or respond.**
> ➢ **Set a step-by-step schedule of what you will be doing and how long it will take.**
> ➢ **Have lists and schedules with you in case you need to refer to them.**
> ➢ **Channel any of your nervous energy with movement or exercise.**
> ➢ **Adjust your perspectives – don't expect too much, and remind yourself to be flexible.**
> ➢ **Talk to yourself – give yourself positive thoughts, talk through difficult situations and remind yourself of the good job you are doing.**
> ➢ **If possible, laugh at yourself and the stressful situation. Laughter will help you relax and feel more comfortable.**
> ➢ **Remind yourself that stress and anxiety will eventually pass, and you will feel better again.**

Everyone experiences stress and anxiety sometimes. You aren't the only one who feels anxious. If anxious thoughts don't go away or if they get worse instead of better, no matter what you do, then this is a problem and you will need to get help from a doctor.

Most of the time when people feel too anxious for too long, they go to the doctor and get medicine or some other treatment prescribed by a doctor. Sometimes a doctor or therapist will try a few things to help the anxiety go away.

Remember, if you have too much anxiety you will need to see your doctor and do what your doctor tells you. Sometimes your doctor will give you medicine for your anxiety. You may need to take medicine every day to stop your scary, anxious thoughts and other anxiety symptoms.

If you aren't sure what causes you stress, an anxiety checklist will help you pin-point situations which cause you the most stress and anxiety. Before taking care of your anxiety or preparing for a possible anxiety attack, it's important to know why you get anxious in the first place.

What Is Causing My Anxiety? Checklist:

1. Some noises bother me _____. This specific noise bothers me: _____.

2. Any loud noises bother me _____.
3. Hot, stuffy environments make me anxious _____. I feel like I can't breathe _____.
4. If too many people are near me _____. I feel crowded _____.
5. I'm afraid someone will touch me _____.
6. If there's too much going on, I feel confused _____.
7. If I'm someplace I don't want to be _____. This place always makes me feel anxious: _____.
8. If I'm with people I don't know _____.
9. If I don't know what to do or say _____.
10. If I don't understand what's happening _____.
11. If I want to leave a place and I can't _____.
12. If I don't know how long I have to be someplace _____.
13. If I'm worried about something I need to do _____.
14. If people are staring at me _____.
15. If too many people are talking to me _____. If more than one person is talking to me at once_____.
16. If there's a change, and I don't know what's next _____.
17. If I can't do something _____. If I don't want to do something _____.
18. If I get scared _____. This scares me: _____.
19. If I need help and don't know who will help me _____.
20. If I'm easily overwhelmed _____ or my senses are overloaded _____.

Too much anxiety is a problem and can be bad for anyone. If you figure out what causes your anxiety, and you can prepare for that possibility, you will have greater control over your anxious thoughts and feelings.

Don't forget to do what the doctor says to control your anxiety in order to feel better in a variety of social situations. Anxiety can be a problem which can make you feel sad, upset and sick. You can feel better when you get the right treatment or medicine.

Dealing with Depression

Everyone feels sad sometimes. You might feel sad about something that happened or didn't happen. Usually you'll feel sad for a day or two, but then you'll feel fine again. Everyone feels sadness sometimes.

If you feel very sad and the sadness seems to take over your life and won't go away, you could have depression.

Depression is an almost constant sadness that can last for several days, weeks or months. Depression can cause you emotional and mental pain. Depression can be exhausting and sometimes physically overwhelming.

When you are depressed, your sadness affects everything you think and do.

If you are depressed for a long time, you might have trouble sleeping, or you may want to sleep all the time. Depression can make you stop eating or eat too much. When you are depressed, you may not care about anything or anybody.

Depression may make you feel like you don't want to do anything at all. You won't even want to do the things you love doing! Depression can make you stop doing things.

If you are very depressed for a long time, you may want to hurt yourself or have thoughts of suicide, such as killing yourself! If you ever think to hurt or kill yourself, you need to get help from a doctor right away!

Depression is like an illness. When you have long or serious times of depression, you need medicine to make you feel better.

Depression is common. Many people can suffer from depression. For most people, depression will happen only occasionally and last a short time. All depression can cause serious problems.

When you experience depression, you need to talk to a doctor and probably get medicine. The doctor will know what to do for your depression.

If you take medicine for depression but don't like the medicine, talk to the doctor before deciding to stop the medicine! If you stop taking your anti-depressant medication, you may suffer even worse problems! Always talk to a doctor if you have problems with your anti-depressant medication. The doctor will figure out what you need. There are lots of different anti-depressant medications, and the doctor will find the right medicine and the right amount for you.

Don't decide if and when you will take medicine on your own. You always need to talk to a doctor first!

Don't use alcohol or illegal drugs to self-medicate, and try to get rid of your depression on your own. Alcohol and drugs may appear to relieve you of your depression temporarily, but any relief you get is not lasting, and it will only make your problem worse instead of better. Alcohol and illegal drugs won't get rid of your depression!

Depression can be a serious problem. Depression is like a blackness that covers you and everything around you. It can make you feel very sad and hopeless. Always talk to a trusted adult and a parent if you are feeling depressed for more than a day or two.

You may think depression will go away on its own, and sometimes it will. Depression can come back again and again, and if this happens, eventually it can become overwhelming! You always need to talk to your doctor when you feel depressed. The doctor will help you figure out how to stop your depression and help you feel good again.

Drug and/or Alcohol Abuse and Addiction

Most people who become addicted to drugs or alcohol first start taking them as a form of self-medication. People who are likely to become addicted to drugs or alcohol are those who drink heavily or use drugs as a way to alleviate anxiety and block out uncomfortable thoughts and memories or to feel happier and more confident about themselves.

Using drugs or alcohol might make you feel better while you use them, but when they wear off, you will usually feel much worse. You may want to take more drugs or alcohol in order to feel better. As you use more and more, your body and mind may become addicted to the drugs or alcohol, and your body will start to feel uncomfortable or painful without them. When you are addicted to drugs or alcohol, your body will need even more of the drugs or alcohol in order to feel good, and this is when overdosing is likely to happen.

Drugs and alcohol are dangerous to your body in large amounts, and taking too much can cause your body to overdose, which can lead to death. A drug or alcohol overdose happens when there is too much (a dangerous amount) of drugs or alcohol in your body. You can even overdose with common medicines that you can buy easily at the store, such as Tylenol and Advil, if you take too much at one time. Always follow the instructions on the medicine bottle to avoid overdosing. Medicines that you buy from a store or get from a doctor will have instructions for you to follow and use safely.

Medications that are prescribed for you by a doctor can help you feel happy and healthy every day, but even prescription medication can be dangerous if you take it inappropriately. When you take medication every day, your body might become very dependent on that medicine, and your body might stop working well once you stop taking it. If you suddenly stop taking your medicine, you might feel angry, anxious, or have trouble sleeping. You could also feel sick or other bad feelings. It is always important to talk to your doctor before you stop using any medicine and work with your doctor to help you stop using medication safely.

Many addictions to illegal drugs start with prescription medication. When you are sick and injured, a doctor may prescribe medication to help you feel less pain. It is important to follow the directions on the prescription bottle and to get rid of any leftover medication when you no longer need it. Do not give your medication to someone else, and do not use medication that was not prescribed for you by a doctor. Incorrectly using prescribed medication and using medication that was not prescribed for you can lead to an addiction. When you have an addiction to prescription drugs, you will look for ways to find or purchase more prescription drugs as well as illegal drugs. Always throw away or safely dispose of old and leftover medication so someone else doesn't find it and use it.

It can be difficult and painful to quit an addiction to prescribed drugs, especially opioids (such as Oxycontin, Vicodin and Percocet) and benzodiazepines (such as Xanax, Valium and Ativan). If you want to quit an addiction to benzodiazepines or opioids, you will need help from a doctor, and you will often need to go to a hospital or rehab clinic. If you want to stop using benzodiazepines, it can be extremely dangerous and can even kill you if you do not have help from a doctor. Methadone is a drug that is often used to help people end addictions to drugs like heroin, but Methadone is also addictive and very dangerous to quit. After getting help from a doctor to detox your body safely from drugs, you will still need help to keep from becoming addicted again. You might want to attend addiction support groups or receive counseling after you quit. Most importantly, you will need to avoid using those drugs ever again!

Illegal drugs are drugs that you don't buy from a store or get from a doctor. Illegal drugs can be very dangerous! Some examples of illegal drugs include heroin, cocaine, methamphetamines, and prescription medications that were not prescribed by a doctor. When a person buys illegal drugs, that person has no way of knowing where the drugs came from, who made them, and what they contain, because they are not regulated by the government. Illegal drugs have no safety instructions. People who make and sell illegal drugs often use different ingredients and mix their drugs with other substances. Sometimes the other substances are more dangerous than the drugs themselves! If you buy an illegal pill or powder, you don't actually know what ingredients are in that pill or powder. The drug content in one dose may be low, and in another it may be much higher. A person might buy and use an illegal drug and feel very good for a while, but when that person goes to buy more of that drug, what he/she buys could be dangerous and make him/her feel very sick. This is how illegal drugs can cause someone to overdose and die. Illegal drugs are dangerous, and if you are caught with them, you will be arrested, and you might go to prison.

Alcohol is not an illegal substance in the U.S., and as long as you are at least 21 years old, you can buy it at many stores. Some common drinks containing alcohol are beer, wine, vodka, whiskey, tequila, gin and rum. It is illegal to buy alcohol and give it to someone under the age of 21, and if you are caught buying alcohol for someone who is under-aged, you could be arrested.

It is okay to drink alcohol, because alcohol is legal to buy and drink. It is common for people to drink a glass of wine or have a beer with a dinner. Drinks like wine can even be healthy for you. You might occasionally drink more alcoholic beverages if you are out with friends or at a party. If you notice that you are often drinking too much alcohol or that you are drinking alcohol every day to help yourself feel better, you should reduce the number of alcoholic beverages you drink. If you notice that it is difficult to reduce the amount of alcohol you drink, you should get help from addiction counselors, addiction groups and doctors.

Many people enjoy drinking alcohol, especially at parties and special events. Alcohol is not naturally addictive, but if you drink a lot of alcohol every day, your body can eventually become addicted to it. An addiction to alcohol often leads to illness and eventual death. Once your body is addicted to alcohol, it is one of the most dangerous and difficult addictions to quit. Quitting an alcohol addiction is extremely painful, and detoxing from alcohol on your own can even cause death! Many people need to go to a hospital to help safely quit an addiction to alcohol. It usually takes months to feel better after ending an alcohol addiction, and in order to be free of your alcohol addiction, you must never drink alcohol again!

Marijuana is a common drug that is completely legal in some states in the U.S. or legal only for medical purposes. In some states, it is still illegal. The laws regarding marijuana vary from state to state, and many states where it is currently illegal are in the process of legalizing it. There is also current and ongoing research that suggests that certain types of marijuana (the kind that contains a low amount of THC and a high amount of CBD) may be very beneficial for safely alleviating anxiety among ASD individuals. It seems likely that, in the future, marijuana will be considered a regulated and legal drug across most of the U.S. If you live in a state where marijuana is currently illegal, you should avoid purchasing it or possessing it, because you could be fined, arrested and possibly sent to prison.

It is extremely dangerous to mix drugs of any kind. Some medicines that you take might make you feel better, but it is often dangerous to take medications with other drugs or alcohol without talking to your doctor. Certain drugs and alcohol are very dangerous when they are in your body at the same time. When you have a prescription from a doctor, your doctor will tell you if you can drink alcohol or take other drugs while you use your medicine. When you buy medicine from a store, the instructions on the bottle or box will often tell you if other medicines and alcohol are dangerous to use at the same time as your medicine. Illegal drugs have no instructions, and it is always very dangerous to mix illegal drugs with any other drugs. You don't know what might happen!

Drug and Alcohol Rules to Follow:

1. You must be 21 years old to buy and drink alcoholic beverages in the U.S.
2. Drinking in moderation (a few alcoholic drinks a week) is typically not considered a problem.
3. Occasionally drinking more at parties is usually okay, but don't ever drink so much that you get drunk or pass out. If you are drinking more than usual, always drink plenty of water and eat food to keep from getting drunk.
4. Don't drive or operate machinery if you have been drinking alcohol.
5. Don't ever mix alcohol and prescription or illegal drugs! Mixing alcohol and drugs could cause death. Most prescription medication will tell you on the bottle if you should not take alcohol while taking that medication.
6. Always follow the directions on any prescription medication you are taking. Don't decide to stop taking medication or increase your dose without first talking to your doctor. If you think you are becoming addicted to your medication, call your doctor.
7. Don't drive or operate machinery if you have taken a prescription pain or sleep drug or any prescription that warns you about driving and operating machinery.
8. Take only your own medication. Don't accept any pills, drugs or medication from someone else.
9. Throw away, or appropriately dispose of, any of your unused medication. Don't save it or give it to anyone.
10. Don't try any illegal drugs! Not only are they illegal, but most of them are dangerous and can be life-threatening.
11. If you become addicted to alcohol or drugs, consult a doctor and possibly an addiction counselor to safely manage and stop your addiction.
12. If you ever suspect you might have a problem with drugs or alcohol, always contact your doctor and possibly an addiction counselor.

Drug and alcohol addictions will eventually lead to many problems. A drug or alcohol addiction can cause you to lose your job and can lead friends and family to not want to be around you. Drug or alcohol addiction can cause you to get into accidents, such as car accidents. When you are addicted to drugs or alcohol, eventually your body will become sick and develop health problems, and you might even die.

Prescription drugs can help you to feel happy and healthy, but it is important to follow your doctor's instructions when using them. When you have questions about increasing, decreasing, stopping or mixing medications, always talk to your doctor or ask a pharmacist first to find out if it's okay.

Remember, never try illegal drugs! Illegal drugs are dangerous and can be addictive. Having or buying them can also get you arrested and sent to prison.

Being addicted to any drugs or alcohol is very dangerous to your health and will cause many problems in your life. Always make smart and safe choices whenever you drink alcohol or take prescription drugs. If you think you have become addicted to drugs or alcohol, talk to your doctor to help you quit your addiction safely. Quitting an addiction to drugs or alcohol can be very difficult, but it is important for your health, safety and happiness.

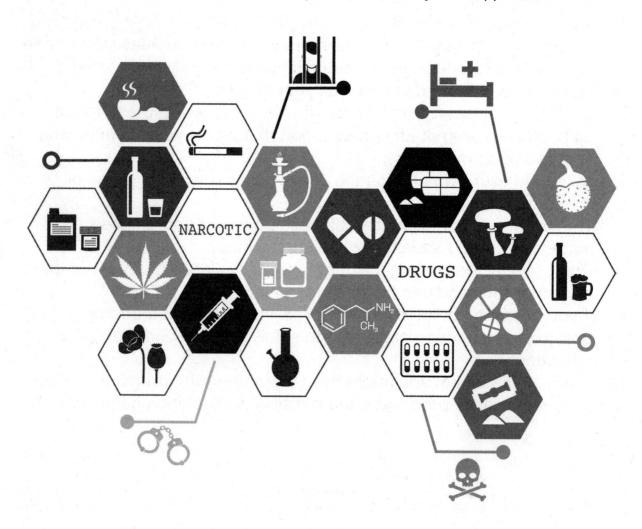

If You Feel Suicidal

When a person feels suicidal, that means he/she is thinking about death and ending his/her life. When people consider committing suicide, it means they want to kill themselves, usually because they feel their life is too painful and they believe death is their only option.

Thinking about suicide is a very serious and desperate state of mind. Most of us can't imagine committing suicide and ending our life. Some people who suffer from severe mental distress can't bear to live anymore and might think suicide is the answer to their problems, but suicide should never be considered. Committing suicide is never the answer to a problem.

There are a number of reasons some people might consider suicide. People might think about death if they have severe and painful depression or if they are unable to see any solution to a difficult and personal problem. Sometimes people are so unhappy with their life that suicide seems like a relief, but suicide is not the solution!

Many people who commit suicide are usually very sad and have been depressed for a long time, and they might think of killing themselves because they can't tolerate living that way any longer. Sometimes people not only feel sad and depressed, but they might also feel helpless or worthless and even hate themselves. All those bad feelings and thoughts might cause them to want to commit suicide. They might believe that being dead would feel better than being alive. No matter how sad and helpless you may be feeling, killing yourself is never the answer to a problem!

Any time someone has thoughts of suicide, even a little bit, we should be alarmed and worried! Thinking about suicide is a very serious and dangerous state of mind! If anyone talks about wanting to die or be dead, that person needs to get help immediately!

If you ever feel so sad and unhappy that you are considering suicide, get help from a trusted adult! Do NOT attempt suicide! Suicide is never the solution. Instead:

1. Tell a trusted adult, parent or guardian immediately that you are thinking of killing yourself. Make sure they understand that you are serious.
2. If you can't immediately contact a trusted adult, call 911 or a 24-hour suicide hotline, like 1-800-SUICIDE or 1-800-273-TALK. You can also call a police station for help.
3. Don't take illegal drugs or alcohol to make yourself feel better. Drugs and alcohol might make you feel better for a short time but will make you feel worse later, and it won't stop your thoughts of dying.
4. Don't hide your suicidal thoughts. Talk to trusted adults about how you are feeling.
5. Don't hurt yourself in any way, even if you hate yourself and are feeling sad or worthless.
6. Anti-depressants and other prescription medications can relieve your severe sadness and help you feel better. A doctor will help you with your depression and anxiety.
7. Doctors, therapists, and social workers can help you feel better about yourself and help you solve your problems.
8. Suicide is against the law! If you or someone you know feels suicidal, you can contact the police for help and prevention.
9. People can't solve their feelings of sadness, worthlessness or helplessness by themselves. You can't control your thoughts of suicide by yourself. You must get help!
10. Remember: suicide is never the solution to your problem, no matter how helpless, hopeless and sad you may feel.

Everyone feels sad and helpless sometimes. We might feel like no one likes us and we are worthless. Sometimes people say terrible things to us to make us doubt ourselves and feel bad.

No matter what anyone tells you to make you feel bad, no matter how big your problem may seem and no matter how very sad you might feel, killing yourself is never the solution. Always get help if you ever have thoughts of suicide!

Staying in a Hospital

Hospitals are not fun places to be in, but sometimes it's necessary to stay in a hospital in order to get better if you are sick. Your doctor will decide if you need to go to a hospital for a procedure or to improve your health.

If your doctor decides it's really important for you to go to a hospital, you should probably obey your doctor's orders. You can ask your doctor why you need to go there and any questions you might have about your procedures. If you are unsure about going to the hospital for a procedure or surgery, you can ask another doctor for a second opinion or ask your parents to contact another doctor for a second opinion. You might still need to go to the hospital, if your parents and doctors decide it's important.

Even though you may be anxious and unhappy about staying in a hospital, it might be easier to think of a hospital as a kind of hotel with strict rules. You can't do whatever you want in a hospital. Your daily routine will change, and you will have little or no privacy. Nurses and doctors will be in to check on you at all hours of the day and night, and you must cooperate with your nurses and doctors while you are in the hospital.

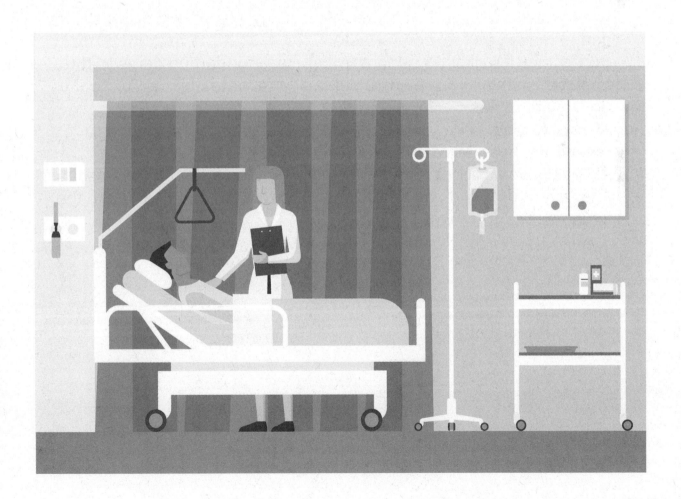

If you have to check into a hospital and you're feeling anxious about it, the following guidelines will help prepare you for your stay:

1. Talk to your doctor and tell him/her all your concerns.
2. Find out as much as you can about all the procedures you will probably have at the hospital. You may not like those procedures, but if they are necessary, try to calmly prepare yourself for them.
3. Write a list of questions to ask the hospital nurses when you arrive.
4. Find out from your doctor about how long you will need to stay.
5. If you want a private room, arrange that with the hospital or your doctor before you arrive.
6. Realize that the hospital has its own rules and routines, and you probably won't be able to change them.
7. You can't change most of the hospital rules, but sometimes you can ask to change one or two things for yourself. Be prepared to make compromises and be flexible.
8. Whenever you feel anxious and upset, tell the hospital staff. Tell them what would help you feel better. Most hospital staff will do what they can to make you feel comfortable.
9. Sometimes it's okay to bring a few special comforting items to the hospital, such as your own pajamas or a favorite object. Talk to the doctor about this.
10. Always explain what you need, and put instructions in writing to remind the hospital staff.
11. Always have a parent or friend with you when you go to the hospital. The parent or friend can talk to the hospital staff and help make the situation better for you.

Remember that the nurses and doctors are there to help you get better. Be cooperative with the hospital staff and try to be as calm as possible, no matter how upset you may feel.

Remember, a hospital stay is not forever. Doctors and nurses want to help you get out of the hospital as soon as possible, so do what you can to get better fast. Cooperate with the doctors and nurses, take all your medicine, follow the rules and directions the hospital staff give you, and before you know it, you will be leaving the hospital and going home.

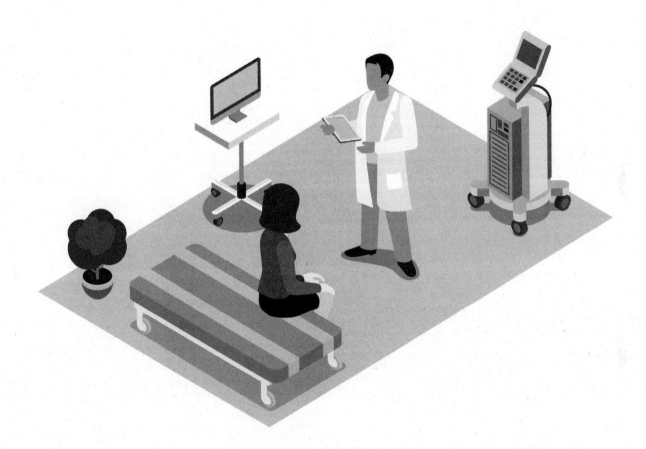

Unit 3: Public Behavior

Introduction to Public Behavior

Be Polite, Not Rude

No Personal Behaviors in Public

Public Bathrooms and Urinal Rules

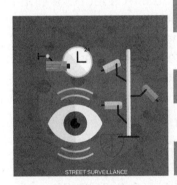

Rules of Private Property

Stalking Is Not Allowed

Staying Calm in Public Places

STREET SURVEILLANCE

Feeling Anxious in Social Situations

Traveling: Buses, Trains, Airplanes

If a Police Officer Stops You

If There Is an Emergency

Introduction to Public Behavior

How you behave in public is often the key to how people will react to you. Everything you do in the presence of others determines how people think about you and act toward you. It's important to be calm and focused and to behave appropriately in public.

The way you behave in public will often dictate where you can go and what you can do. This is typically an unwritten rule, one that most people understand and follow. Most people know to behave with an appropriate level of politeness in public. We know we need to exhibit calm behavior, even when we might be very upset or anxious. There will always be people who behave inappropriately in public, and everyone near them is well aware of that bad or inappropriate behavior.

When an individual with autism has very difficult behavior and can't control his/her actions in public, it automatically limits the places he/she can go. It's important for all individuals with autism to follow the rules of appropriate public behavior in order to ensure their safety and allow them more access to a variety of places, people and events.

We all like to know what to expect in a new situation, and how to behave. Most people will carefully observe and copy the behavior of others if they aren't sure what to do and what would be considered appropriate behavior. Many people on the autism spectrum don't typically know that they should observe the specific behavior of others to recognize how to act in a new situation. Even if they do observe the behaviors of others in their vicinity, they might have a difficult time understanding the behavior exhibited by others. Furthermore, they may have a hard time determining appropriate vs. inappropriate behavior from others and effectively copying the appropriate behavior.

For the purposes of this section of information, anywhere outside of a person's home, and especially in the presence of other people, is considered public.

When it comes to people with autism and their public behavior, many people immediately think of meltdowns and anxiety attacks. And these are certainly areas of concern. It is critical that teens and adults with ASD learn to self-calm and manage any of their out-of-control behaviors if they want to get out in public and participate in a variety of activities with others. If an individual with autism has frequent meltdowns in public, is aggressive toward others and destroys property, he/she will not be able to continue to go to public places, especially if his/her behavior meltdowns are random and uncontrollable. That will also limit his/her ability to make friends and do a variety of enriching and enjoyable activities. Consequently, the chances that he/she will get a job and do worthwhile activities in the community will likely disappear. The same can be said about intense anxiety, which may lead to meltdowns or the inability to tolerate many environments. When it comes to being in public places, managing anxiety and out-of-control behavior is essential.

When you are out in public, either alone or with a group of peers, you are required to adhere to safety procedures and rules. We all need to pay attention to posted signs and warnings we see out in public, especially if they constitute a safety precaution. Along those lines, individuals with autism need to recognize and know how to respond to potential dangers in public as well as how to behave during emergencies.

Teens and adults with autism who may walk or travel in their community need to be prepared to interact with police and/or security personnel. An individual with ASD might simply be walking in the park, but if a police officer stops him/her for whatever reason, they must know the rules and cooperate with the police. A police officer is not likely to recognize that someone has autism. If, for instance, an individual with ASD became scared and ran away or aggressed toward a police officer, the consequences could be disastrous.

We all want our teens and young adults with autism to have access to a variety of environments and public places. Being able to comfortably go to many different places, especially on their own or with peers, allows teens and adults with ASD to become more confident and independent and to do more things, meet more people and enrich their lives.

Tips for Teachers/Instructors:

- Take frequent field trips to a variety of community places.
- Teach self-calming and behavior management.
- Practice and role-play public behavior in support groups. Teach them what to say and do in a variety of situations.
- Emphasize safety procedures in public places. Teach them to recognize or read signs in the community and follow the directions or warning on the sign.
- As students become familiar with public places in the community, reduce the prompts and hands-on support you give them. Give them a chance to demonstrate what they can do on their own.
- Help students be confident and as independent as possible in public.

Tips for Parents:

- Take your child out to a variety of places from an early age, including public bathrooms.
- Help your child become comfortable with public transportation.
- Get your son/daughter familiar with a number of people, not just family members.
- Teach your child how to be polite and practice doing so in public.
- Make sure your child recognizes and understands important signs, especially warning signs, he/she might see in public, and demonstrate/ practice how to follow them.
- Don't tolerate or manage your child's bad behavior! Your child needs to learn to manage his/her own behavior and learn strategies to self-calm.
- Help your child learn to make the correlation that good behavior means access to more public places.
- Devise signals or cues that your child can use with you to indicate when he/she is overwhelmed and needs to leave a public place. Push your child to tolerate more new places, but don't push to the point that he/she has a major meltdown.
- Help your child learn to enjoy being in a variety of public places.

Tips for Teens and Young Adults with ASD:

- Don't stay home or on your computer too much. Challenge yourself to go to a variety of different places on a regular basis.
- Go to social or public events with friends, co-workers, and peers. Don't only go places with parents and caregivers.
- Before you go anywhere new, learn as much as you can about where you are going, how you will get there, what to expect, who you might see, and how long you will be there.
- Have a plan and strategies for when you feel anxious, fearful, or overwhelmed in a public area. Let friends and family members help with your plans and self-calming strategies.
- Always carry a cell phone with you when you are out in public, whether you are alone or in a group.
- Be aware of any signs as well as any potential dangers when you are out in public places.
- If a police officer stops you, tell him/her you have autism, and make sure to use the word, "autism." Do this before you become too anxious and exhibit any out-of-control behaviors, and do this before the police officer assumes you are a dangerous person.

Be Polite, Not Rude

Most people expect and appreciate polite behavior from others in public. When you are polite to others, people are more likely to respond favorably and be polite to you as well.

Being polite shouldn't be difficult, and it will typically make a big difference when interacting with others. Simple actions such as smiling at people, saying "please" when asking for something and "thank you" when someone brings you something or does a service for you will make people smile and appreciate you. People also appreciate it when you say "you're welcome" after they thank you for something. Saying "please," "thank you" and "you're welcome" and smiling are polite ways to interact with others at home, and especially in public.

If you are rude and demanding of people, they will usually respond in a rude and angry way toward you. And if you have a frowning or angry look on your face when you meet or interact with people, they are likely to frown back at you.

Making eye contact is a way to be polite. When people are talking to you – friends, co-workers, teachers, neighbors and even strangers – it is usually customary to look at their faces or make eye contact. Making eye contact, even just occasionally, shows people that you are listening to them and interested in what they are saying. Sometimes making eye contact can be difficult and uncomfortable for you. Making occasional eye contact may make a difference when interacting with others. If looking at someone's eyes during a conversation is difficult, you can look at their whole face instead. This will still let people feel as though you are listening to them without causing you too much discomfort. People like it when you look them in the face or eyes, even just briefly.

It is important to keep personal space when facing someone. When we approach people and talk to them face-to-face, we need to keep enough personal space between us. Personal space is the space you keep between yourself and another person, usually when you are face-to-face. Most people are comfortable with a space of two-to-three feet, unless you need to briefly get closer to whisper or say something for only that person to hear. Even if you step closer to say something confidential, be sure and step back and leave a two-to-three-feet space after you finish whispering.

People become alarmed and uncomfortable if you stand too close to them. Standing a foot in front of someone is too close. The two-to-three-feet rule is especially important if you are talking to anyone who isn't a close friend or family member. People don't mind so much if you are very close to them in a cramped place, such as an elevator, as long as you aren't face-to-face with them in a cramped situation.

There are many things people do that are considered rude. Making rude noises, swearing, saying insults or mean things to people and doing gross or nasty things to others, or near others, are considered offensive. Pushing people aside or knocking them down, even accidentally is rude, and you should apologize for your rude behavior if you do this. People will not be happy and may even get angry at you if you behave offensively and rudely to them.

Rules of Politeness Include:

1.   Smile at people you pass or meet.
2.   Say "please," "thank you" and "you're welcome" to people you know, as well as acquaintances and strangers, when it is appropriate.
3.   Say "Hi" and "how are you" when you meet someone you know, and say "bye, nice talking to you," when you finish talking and start to leave.
4.   Immediately apologize anytime you do something rude or offensive, even if it was an accident.
5.   Make eye contact or turn and look at the face of someone who says something to you.
6.   Occasionally make eye contact, smile and nod your head to show you are listening to the person speaking to you.
7.   Keep a personal space of two-to-three feet between you and someone you are talking to face-to-face (personal space is usually not needed with family members and loved ones).
8.   Hold the door open for someone walking behind you, especially if that person is holding something.
9.   Offer to help a person if he/she drops something or needs a hand.
10. Don't make rude noises or insult anyone.
11. Don't swear at anyone or say mean, hateful things, including family members and people you love.
12. Don't offend anyone with gross or nasty behavior.
13. Don't push people aside or knock them down, even if you are in a hurry.
14. Don't make rude or threatening gestures at anyone.

Not everyone you meet will be polite. In fact, some people you meet will be rude and offensive. If someone is rude and offensive to you, try to ignore it and move away from the rude person. That's how most people react when someone is being rude or offensive.

Remember, people are more likely to be polite and friendly to you if you are polite and friendly to them. It is usually a good rule to be polite to everyone, especially people you pass or talk to in public.

No Personal Behaviors in Public

There are many actions that everyone does which are private and personal and shouldn't be done in public. Some things we do in private would be considered gross, unhygienic or just inappropriate in front of other people.

Almost everyone does these activities in private, because if you did them in public, people would probably be disgusted and upset. Gross, unhygienic and inappropriate behavior in public will turn people off! If you do these things in public, not only will people avoid you, but peers may choose not to be your friend.

Sometimes we might accidentally do something people might think is disgusting, like burping or farting. If we burp or fart in front of others, we simply need to apologize, and try not to do it again. Sometimes when we fart we might be able to pretend it just didn't happen and not mention it or apologize for it. Many people do this, and that's okay. Every time we obviously burp or fart in front of others, we should apologize, and simply say "excuse me" or "sorry." Most of the time people will excuse burps and farts, because we can't always control them.

Other, more purposeful gross or inappropriate behaviors won't usually be forgiven or excused. If we do gross, inappropriate behaviors on purpose, people will be disgusted and avoid us. Sometimes your friends may decide not to be your friend if they see you doing a gross, inappropriate behavior.

The following private, personal behaviors should not be done in public, especially while others are watching:

- Picking your nose
- Eating snot from your nose (this is very gross and can cause you to be sick)
- Eating or licking dirty or gross things, or licking your fingers after touching something gross/dirty
- Spitting
- Wiping your nose on your clothing
- Picking your teeth
- Cleaning or picking wax from your ears
- Picking or cleaning your toe nails
- Picking a scab from your skin
- Putting your hands down your pants
- Touching or rubbing your genitals or breasts, even over your clothing
- Scratching your butt
- Touching feces or urine (this is not something you should ever do intentionally, because it is very dirty and unhygienic)
- Removing clothing, such as shoes, socks, shirt, skirt, a dress and pants, in a public area, when no one else is removing any clothing, or where removing clothing is not allowed

Since many of these behaviors are disgusting and unhygienic, we must always wash our hands with soap and water after touching something gross and dirty.

Most people do some of these inappropriate and unhygienic behaviors in private and don't talk about them. As long as these behaviors are done in private, with hand washing afterwards as needed, and no one talks about them, it is okay and none of anyone's business.

Public Bathrooms and Urinal Rules

Many people dislike using public bathrooms because they may smell bad or smell different from what they are used to. You might not like the toilets or toilet paper in a public bathroom. You may find using a public bathroom, and especially a portable toilet, unacceptable and extremely uncomfortable. If that is the case, you will need to plan your trips carefully, and always use your own toilet before going somewhere. Sometimes you won't have a choice, and you will need to use a public bathroom. You may want to check out a public bathroom before you need to use it to see if the bathroom will be acceptable for you and if it has what you need.

Public bathrooms are not like personal, private bathrooms in your home. Even though people typically use a public bathroom to use a toilet or urinal, most people are careful to be modest and discreet in a public bathroom, because usually you will not be in a public bathroom by yourself.

It is not okay to display gross, unhygienic behavior in a public bathroom, especially when others can see you. If you need to change clothes, adjust your clothing, or pick your nose, you need to do this in a bathroom stall with the door closed.

Sexual activity with yourself or others is also not appropriate in a public bathroom, where other people can come in and possibly see or hear you. If you perform a sexual activity in a public bathroom, you might even be arrested for lewd and indecent behavior! Even if you engage in sexual activity in a bathroom stall, where no one can see you, it is still illegal and could get you in trouble.

When Using a Urinal in a Public Bathroom:

- Be as modest and discreet as possible.
- Never sit in a urinal. Urinals are not for sitting! You should only stand in front of a urinal when using it.
- Most men and boys know never to drop their pants and underwear to the floor when using a urinal. This is considered very inappropriate and a possible danger to you if you expose your naked butt.
- You should stand close to the urinal and take down your pants only as far as you need to, in order to urinate (pee).
- It is also inappropriate to purposefully stand next to someone using a urinal, especially if the person is a stranger and there are other empty urinals further away from him to choose from.
- It is considered very rude and inappropriate to watch someone peeing at a urinal. If you watch someone peeing, that person will think you are looking at his naked genitals and will likely get angry or upset.

Most bathrooms in public places are safe to use. Public bathrooms aren't places you want to stay in for very long. Most people in a public bathroom will do their business, such as use a toilet, wash and dry their hands, then leave the bathroom. Sometimes people who want to do harm to you or others could be loitering in a public bathroom. Sometimes people sell drugs or try to engage in sex with others in a public bathroom. If you suspect someone is there to bother or harm you or if something illegal is happening, leave the bathroom immediately!

Not everyone enjoys using a public bathroom or an outhouse toilet. Sometimes those bathrooms can be dirty and stinky. Using a public bathroom is something we may have to do when we need a toilet. As long as you follow the rules for safe and modest use of a public bathroom, including washing your hands after using the toilet, your experience should be just fine.

Rules of Private Property

Private property refers to anything that isn't yours. Parents and family members may let you take and use things in your home that don't belong to you, but other people might get upset or angry if you use their things.

If something doesn't belong to you, you should ask permission from the owner to take or use it. Even if you only want to borrow something for a short time, you need to ask permission before taking it.

People are likely to get upset and angry if something of theirs is taken without permission. This is typically true wherever you go. Unless someone in authority or the owner offers you something or tells you to take what you want, you should assume permission is needed before taking and using anything that isn't yours.

Stealing is illegal and could get you arrested, especially if you steal something from a store or business. Stealing from friends, family members, classmates, neighbors and co-workers might not get you arrested, but it's still wrong, and consequently stealing may cause you to lose friends and possibly your job. At the very least, it may cause people to distrust you.

It's also important not to damage or destroy items or property belonging to someone else. This would include gardens, playground equipment, cars, toys, pets, furniture, walls and windows, someone's clothing and basically anything not belonging to you.

Some Private Property Rules:

- Don't take and eat food that doesn't belong to you without permission.
- Don't open packages or eat food from a store without paying for it.
- Don't steal or conceal items you find in any building, home, or outside property, including any money that doesn't belong to you.
- Don't damage, deface or destroy any items not belonging to you, including public property.
- Don't trespass on property that doesn't belong to you or your family.
- Don't use anything belonging to someone else without asking permission, including things you find outside on someone else's property.
- Don't harm or take animals, including pets, belonging to someone else.
- Ask permission to use any food, property, items or equipment that isn't yours.

You need to respect the property and personal items belonging to others. Be careful not to take or damage anything belonging to someone else. If you want to borrow or use something, you need to ask permission. Just because you ask permission doesn't mean that you will be allowed to use something. A person may refuse to let you use something belonging to him/her, and that's okay. A person can decide what he/she wants to do with things that belong to him/her, and sometimes that includes not letting you or others use it.

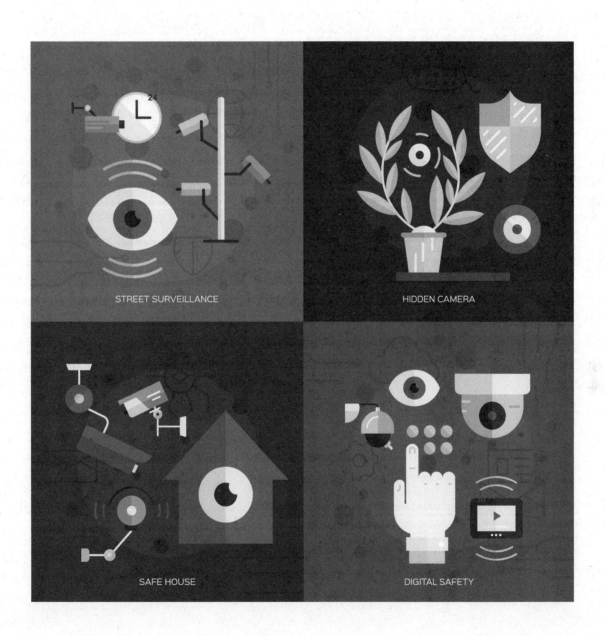

STREET SURVEILLANCE

HIDDEN CAMERA

SAFE HOUSE

DIGITAL SAFETY

Stalking Is Not Allowed

Repeatedly following, bothering or harassing a person either physically or on social media is called stalking. Stalking is typically seen as threatening and aggressive, and in most places it is illegal.

Stalking is any unwanted behavior and attention given to someone who doesn't want or encourage it. You may mean well and want to show a person how much you like them, but if your behavior causes the person to become anxious, fearful or angry, then what you are doing is stalking, and stalking is not allowed.

Examples of stalking include sending gifts, writing love or hate letters, calling a person frequently, waiting outside a person's house, watching a person and following them to a variety of places when they don't want you to. These days, someone is more likely to stalk a person online, through social media, by constantly watching you online and commenting on things you post.

You might think that it isn't stalking if you like a person, or have a good interest in someone. No matter how you feel about someone, even if you like a person very much and want a relationship with that person, if the person you are spending time watching and following doesn't want you bothering him/her, then your attention is considered stalking.

Even gifts, flowers, friendly calls and letters are considered threatening if the person you are sending them to does NOT want them. If you send something to a person you like or watch and follow that person, even on social media, and that person ignores you or tells you to stop, you need to stop. Stop sending gifts and letters, making phone calls and constantly following someone on social media if that person ignores you or tells you to stop. If you don't stop, then you are stalking him/her.

Stalking is not allowed for anyone. If you find that someone is stalking you, tell them to stop immediately. If they don't stop, contact the police and report any stalking behavior.

Staying Calm in Public Places

Usually the hardest part about being in a public place with lots of different and sometimes overwhelming stimuli is trying to stay calm.

Public places can be noisy and crowded. Sometimes public places can be confusing or scary. You might get anxious, upset or angry in a public place, such as a store, a restaurant, movie theaters, a school, a library, on a bus or in a park. Even if you get upset, it's not okay to have a meltdown.

If you know you will be going someplace stressful and you think you may become upset, make a list of all the things that might make you feel anxious and cause you to stress out. Have someone write a Social Story™ with you to help you understand the situation better, recognize expected behaviors and learn how to cope with difficulties. Anticipate what would make you upset, and figure out how to manage it. Parents and friends can help you problem-solve and handle tough, stressful situations.

Above all, it's important to stay calm in public and not get upset or have a meltdown. Even if you are feeling angry, distressed, worried, sad or anxious, you need to practice appropriate behavior in public. It may be okay to have a tantrum or meltdown in private, but it's not okay to show those behaviors in public, especially when you aren't by yourself.

There are consequences for bad, out-of-control behavior in public. Bad behavior in public will cause other people to avoid you and maybe get angry with you. You might get thrown out of a restaurant, store or place of business if you have very bad behavior. You might even be arrested if your behavior is especially rude or dangerous, or if you hurt someone or damage property.

Avoid These Inappropriate Behaviors in Public:

- ➢ Don't scream or shout, and don't talk too loudly.
- ➢ Don't run away from your friends or family.
- ➢ Don't throw yourself on the floor or ground.
- ➢ Don't throw things, especially at anyone.
- ➢ Don't destroy things or property, especially anything that doesn't belong to you.
- ➢ Don't hit, kick or try to hurt others, including parents or caregivers.
- ➢ Don't purposely hurt yourself.
- ➢ Don't swear or yell rude or hateful things at anyone.
- ➢ Don't threaten anyone with harm.
- ➢ Don't cry or act hysterical. This will upset people near you.
- ➢ Don't hold or point a weapon, such as a knife, a stick, your fist or a gun (even a play gun) at anyone.
- ➢ Don't make threatening moves towards anyone.

Behaving badly or inappropriately in public might startle or scare people. Someone may think you are dangerous and a threat to others. Authorities or the police may be called to restrain or remove you.

When Distressed, Try Some Self-Calming Techniques:

- Hold and use a small de-stressing item, such as a stress ball, a small squeeze toy, or another familiar, calming item.
- Sit down and place your hands on your lap.
- Close your eyes and block out overwhelming things you see.
- With eyes closed, picture a happy place or a favorite movie in your head.
- Take several long, slow breaths until you feel your body relax.
- Listen to your favorite relaxing music, or think of your favorite music in your head (you may want to wear ear buds and listen to music on an iPod).
- Remind yourself to ignore those things that make you mad or scared.
- Silently tell yourself positive, reassuring messages, such as "I can do this!" or "I'm ok, I'll be able to leave soon, I can ignore this."
- Hug yourself tightly.
- Press your hands or fingertips together.
- Move away from anything that is stressful or overwhelming.
- Take a walk.
- Go to a quiet place until you feel calmer.
- Speak quietly (a quiet voice will make you feel calmer).
- Count in your head slowly to 10 or to 20 or higher until you feel calm.
- If you are still upset but feeling calmer and able to talk, tell your friends, parent or caregiver that you are overwhelmed and stressed out and that you need to leave.

There are many techniques and strategies for self-calming. Find the strategies that work for you and practice them in a calm environment. Don't practice your self-calming techniques in a stressful environment unless you know they will work for you and you can do them successfully.

Everyone feels anxious and stressed out sometimes. If you are prepared for a stressful situation, you know what to expect and you have strategies to manage your stress, you should do fine in public places. Remember that the stress and anxiety you feel won't last forever. Soon those feelings will be gone, and you will feel calm again.

Feeling Anxious in Social Situations

Social situations can make most people feel anxious, especially in an unfamiliar or uncomfortable situation. A social situation is any place where people gather for an event or activity. In a social situation, people are typically with others they know or want to get to know. People are expected to interact with each other by talking and standing near others in a social gathering. A social situation can have a few people or many people, and it may include people you know as well as people you don't know well or not at all.

If you know you will feel anxious in a social situation, try to go with a friend, or ask a friend to meet you there. Social situations are always better if you have a friend with you. A friend will help you feel comfortable and will be there to talk to you. It's easier to meet new people and talk to people when you have a friend with you to support and help you. This is true for everyone! Very few people like going to social events where they don't know anyone and don't know what to expect.

If you need or want to go to a social event, but you know you will feel anxious, make a list of all the things you think might cause you anxiety before you go. Look at your list and figure out how you will handle every possible anxiety-producing situation with a trusted adult or friend.

Learn as much as you can about the social situation you are going to. For example, is this a dinner with family or friends at someone's house? Is this a sports event? A birthday party? A church gathering? A large, outdoor party? A restaurant gathering? A workplace meeting or a place to hang out with co-workers? A support group or club meeting? A wedding or funeral? Find out about where you are going, who will be there, what you will be doing, how long it will last, and how you will dress for this occasion. The more you know about a situation, the more comfortable and less anxious you will feel there. Have a trusted adult write a Social Story™ about a social event you will be attending to help you prepare for it.

Think about how you will act in each situation. Make a list of things you can say or do with the help of a friend or adult. Practice and role-play with friends or adults to help you prepare what you can say and do in a specific situation. When you are at an event, observe what others are saying and doing, and try to keep your interactions similar to theirs.

In social situations, it's important to look and act like those around you. Be sure you are dressed appropriately for the occasion. Ask a friend, party host, or parent what you should wear before going to a social event.

Many people with ASD find that stimming helps them calm down. The more anxious you are, the more stimming you are likely to do. Stimming is fine, but you need to stim like a neuro-typical. Many neuro-typicals stim, but their stimming is considered acceptable and appropriate.

Some Appropriate Neurotypical Stimming Examples:

- Tapping and clicking pens or pencils
- Tapping your foot (if sitting)
- Holding and rubbing an object, such as a glass or cup
- Drumming your fingers softly on your leg, chair or table
- Rubbing your fingers together
- Twirling and twisting your hair (this works better if you are a girl)
- Twisting rings on your fingers
- Arranging or touching a few objects near you on a table
- Bouncing your leg, while sitting
- Gentle, slow rocking or side-to-side movement
- Humming softly
- Holding, looking at and fiddling with your cell phone

Remember to keep your stims subtle, quiet, calm and brief. Don't stim constantly. Stop stimming after a few minutes, wait calmly for a few minutes, then begin stimming again if you need to. Keep up this pattern of neuro-typical stimming while you're in social situations. Remember to take breaks from stimming, because some people will notice if you stim too much or for too long.

You may become overwhelmed in social situations and need a brief escape to calm down. Plan where you will go to get away from others. Be sure you excuse yourself from the group you are with, and calmly walk to the bathroom, take a brief walk down a hallway, go outside (if appropriate), or go to a designated room, where you know you can be alone. Don't wait until your anxiety is out of control and you are too panicked or upset to manage it! Take care of your anxiety calmly, before it becomes too much to handle.

If you become so anxious and overwhelmed that you have to leave before a social occasion is over, excuse yourself from the group, thank the host (if appropriate), and leave as calmly as possible. If you anticipate that this may happen, have a code word or phrase that your friend or host knows to let them know you are too anxious and need to leave. When you tell your friend or host the code word or phrase, they will help you leave as quickly and calmly as possible, without anyone else knowing.

Almost everyone feels some anxiety in new or uncomfortable situations. Be as prepared as you can before you go to any social situation. The more prepared you are, the less anxious you will be.

Traveling: Buses, Trains, Airplanes

When you are out walking, biking, driving or otherwise traveling, it's always important to pay attention to signs and obey them. Most signs in public places, such as streets, parks, and buildings, as well as private property signs are there for our safety, or to instruct us as to what we should or should not do.

Some signs are warnings, which may result in serious consequences if ignored. You should be especially careful and follow the instructions of any sign that has the word "warning," "caution," "emergency" or "danger" on it. If you don't obey traffic signs and anything involving personal property, you could be ticketed or arrested. Signs are put up for a reason. Pay attention to signs you see, especially if they include you and your actions.

Traveling by Bus

Most of the time when you travel by bus, there is no assigned seating. You can usually sit wherever there's an empty seat. When you enter a public bus, you may need to pay the driver or present him/her with your ticket. Most buses that travel in a city require exact change, which means you need to be prepared to pay the exact amount required when you board the bus.

Since there are usually no assigned seats on a bus, choose a seat, either a window or aisle seat that is empty. If the bus is almost full, it may be necessary to sit next to another person. If so, be polite (smile and say "Hi") when you take your seat, but don't attempt to talk with the person next to you if you don't know that person. Most people on a bus would prefer to be quiet, and not talk to strangers. If you sit next to someone you don't know, keep yourself and your belongings within the space of your own seat.

If the bus is completely full, you may need to stand until a seat becomes available. Hold onto a metal bar or pole and balance yourself as well as possible. Try not to bump into others. Public transportation buses stop frequently, and people will get on and off the bus at each stop. Be familiar with when you will need to get off, and pay attention if your stop is announced. If you are traveling on a bus without a friend or family member, it's your responsibility to know when it's time to get off the bus. It's not likely anyone will tell you when to get off the bus. When you know your bus stop is coming up, stand, take your things and move toward the exit so you are ready to get off the bus quickly and safely.

Traveling by Train

Traveling by train is often similar to traveling by bus. If you are taking a commuter train, there is no assigned seating, and you can choose any seat that's empty. You will need to get a ticket before you get on the train or buy one from the conductor when he comes through the train to check passengers for tickets. Like a bus, the train will probably make many stops, with people getting on and off. If you are traveling on an Amtrak train, you will usually have an assigned seat or an assigned room.

Many train doors open and close automatically. There are often many people getting on and off a train at most stops. In the case of commuter trains, the passengers are usually in a rush and moving quickly. Be careful when you get on or off a train. The steps can be steep and the doors will often close quickly.

Like a bus, if the train car is almost full, you might need to sit next to someone. The rules for the bus are usually the same for the train. Be polite, but keep quiet, and stay within the personal space of your seat, including your belongings.

Most trains have a bathroom, but it won't be like your bathroom at home. When you close the door to the train bathroom, you may need to lock it by sliding a knob to the left or right. Sometimes the lights won't come on until you slide the knob. If you are unsure about how to use the bathroom, have a friend or family member show you how to lock and unlock the door before you attempt to do it on your own. It can be easy to get stuck and have a hard time getting out of this type of bathroom. Unless you really need to use the bathroom, you may want to avoid the bathroom on a train.

Traveling by Airplane

Airports are probably the most confusing and difficult places to be when you are traveling. Most airports are large, and there are usually many people in them. If you feel confused, anxious, frustrated and scared at an airport, you won't be the only one feeling that way. Many people feel anxious, frustrated and even agitated at an airport. It is always best to go to an airport with a friend, family member or trusted adult, because airports are especially stressful and confusing, and you may need someone with you who can explain the rules and procedures. Get to the airport in plenty of time, usually one to two hours before your flight, so you have enough time to go through security and find your gate.

Airports are very strict about their procedures, and you will need to follow the rules at the airport. If you don't follow the rules at an airport, you will not be allowed on the plane. First, you will need to find your airline, get tickets and check bags, if you are bringing luggage. Usually that involves waiting your turn in line.

After you have your ticket, you will need to go through airport security. Airport security is stressful for everyone. Again, you will need to wait in line and have your ticket and ID ready for a security officer to check. When you go through security, you will need to put some of your belongings in a plastic bin on a conveyor belt. Your watch, phone, wallet, purse, coat, computer, belt, and sometimes your shoes must be put in the plastic bin and sent through the security conveyor belt.

You will have to walk through a security doorway, and if you are wearing anything metal, the doorway will probably make beeping sounds. Pay attention to what the security people tell you to do, and follow their instructions. Sometimes it is necessary for a security person to touch you to be sure you aren't carrying or hiding any weapons. Try to stay calm during this procedure and let them do their job. Don't argue or fight with the security person. If you do, you won't be allowed through the security gate, and if you get angry or upset, you might be removed from the airport or even get arrested. Getting through security is probably the hardest thing you will have to do at the airport.

Once you are through security, you will need to gather your things from the conveyor belt and walk to your gate. Your airline ticket will tell you the gate and flight number for your plane. Look at the signs around you, and go in the direction of your gate. Your airline gate may be close by or a long walk away. Each airport is different, and you might not know how far away your gate is until you reach it.

When you reach your airline gate, check to see if the gate and flight number match the ones on your ticket. Check to see if your plane is leaving on time or if there has been a delay or gate change. This is important, especially if the change means you have to go to a different gate. You may have to wait a long time before boarding (getting on) your plane. If you have time before boarding, you might want to get something to eat or drink, buy a magazine and use the toilet.

Your ticket will tell you when they will start boarding people on your plane. You may notice a group number on your ticket. People in group 1 are generally boarded first, and people in group 4 or 5 often get to board the plane last. It usually takes about 30 minutes to get everyone on the plane and get their luggage stowed appropriately.

Everyone has an assigned seat on a plane, and you need to sit in your assigned seat; you can find your seat number on your ticket. If you can't handle sitting in the middle seat of a plane, try to get a window or aisle seat when you buy your ticket. Remember, you usually can't change seats once you get on the plane. When you reach your seat you will need to put any luggage you have in an overhead compartment, or if it's small enough, under your seat. Flight attendants can help you with this.

Airplanes have seat belts, and you will be instructed to wear yours for most of the flight. Once everyone is on board the plane, the flight attendants will explain the safety rules and other procedures.

The hardest part about flying in an airplane is the takeoff and landing. It might feel uncomfortable and scary. You may want to chew gum during takeoff, because the change in air pressure may make your ears pop or hurt a little. An airplane is very loud when it's flying. Most people get used to the loud noise after a while, but if you can't get used to it, consider bringing noise-reducing headphones with you.

The bathroom on an airplane is very small and confusing. The toilet and sink are very different from your toilet or bathroom at home. Like the bathroom on a train, the door and lock can be difficult to operate. The lock will usually slide from the left to the right and can be tricky. There are many signs and instructions in an airplane bathroom, and you should read them carefully in order to know what you need to do. It is usually a good idea to use the washroom in the airport before getting on the airplane, because the airplane bathroom may be too small and difficult for you to manage.

Flight attendants will show you how to use the controls near your airplane seat. Flight attendants will also bring you a drink and sometimes a snack during the flight. If you have a problem during the flight, you can ask the flight attendant for help.

The most important thing to remember is to stay calm during the flight. Bring a magazine or book to read or a game to play during the flight to keep you calm and focused. You can bring your own snacks, if you want. Try not to get anxious or agitated on the plane. If you freak out and have a meltdown on a plane, there's a good chance that security people on the plane may need to restrain you during the flight.

Almost everyone gets anxious, frustrated and stressed at an airport and sometimes on a plane. Do what you need to do to stay calm while in an airport or on an airplane, but always remember to follow the rules!

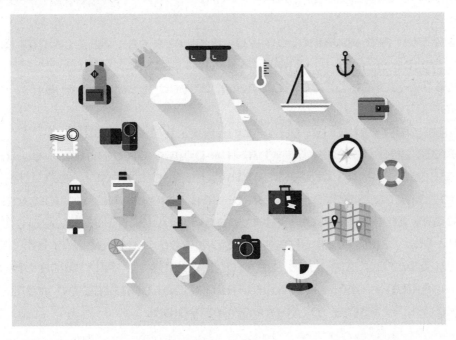

If a Police Officer Stops You

Sometimes if you are out walking, riding a bike or driving in a car, a police officer might decide to stop you. The police officer may wonder where you are going and what you are doing. A police officer may need to remind you of the rules and what you should do.

Police officers want everyone to be safe. Sometimes a police officer will stop people to make sure they are being safe, following the rules and doing a good job. A police officer in a car might turn on his/her flashing lights and siren. If that happens, you need to pull your car to the side of the road and turn off the car. If you are walking or riding a bike, you need to stop and wait for the police officer to approach you.

A police officer might want to ask a few questions or give you instructions. He/she will often ask you for identification, a driver's license or your address. It's important to cooperate with a police officer and do as he/she asks.

If you are ever concerned that the person stopping you is not a police officer, you can politely ask the officer to show you his/her identification, such as a police badge. Most of the time you will know someone is a police officer by the police car, police uniform and police badge.

If Stopped or Pulled Over by a Police Officer:

1. Stop immediately! Stop walking, safely pull your car over to the side of the road or stop whatever you are doing. You should never run from a police officer.
2. Turn and face the police officer. You need to keep your hands at your side, or up in the air if the officer asks you to raise your hands.
3. If you are driving a car, keep your hands on the steering wheel until the officer allows you to get your driver's license and car insurance.
4. Don't put your hands in your pockets or in a bag or a purse unless the officer allows you to. Police officers always need to see your hands.
5. Whether you are walking, on a bike or in a car, wait calmly and quietly for the police officer to come to you.
6. Wait for the police officer to speak to you first, and answer all his/her questions truthfully.
7. Be polite. Don't start an argument with a police officer!
8. Cooperate and do exactly what the police officer tells you to do.
9. If the officer doesn't understand you or gets angry with you, you will need to explain that you have autism. This is very important! If you exhibit any anxious or out-of-control behavior, the police officer may assume you are a dangerous person. You must calmly tell the police that you have autism. Use the word, "autism." All police officers will recognize that word. The police might not understand words like "Asperger's," "Aspie" or "non-neurotypical."

10. If a police officer decides to give you a ticket, don't argue or get angry. Getting angry with the police will only get you into more trouble and possibly arrested!
11. If the police officer decides to arrest you for whatever reason, you must cooperate and try to stay calm. If the police put handcuffs on you, don't fight him/her! Stay calm and let the police do what they need to do.
12. Once you get to the police station, tell any police officers who are talking to you or holding you that you have autism. Call your parents or guardian as soon as the officers allow you to, and make sure your parents/guardian are able to come to the police station to answer police questions and help you with the process.

It is always important to cooperate with police officers. If you do something wrong, illegal or act disrespectful, a police officer might give you a ticket or even arrest you.

If you are arrested, you must calmly cooperate with the police. If the police think you are a danger to others or that you have a weapon and plan to fight or hurt someone, they will restrain you and could possibly hurt you!

A police officer wants everyone, including you, to obey the laws and be safe. Remember to always cooperate and follow the rules when a police officer stops you.

If There Is an Emergency

Emergencies can occur anywhere and are usually sudden and unexpected. Even when people know about possible emergencies, they usually aren't prepared for them when they happen.

Any time there is an emergency, schedules and routine activities are disrupted. Because of an emergency, people may need to do something unusual, such as stop what they are doing and leave a location immediately.

There are many different types of and causes for emergencies. Floods, wildfires, earthquakes, tornados, landslides, and various severe storms are types of natural disasters which usually result in people in those affected areas needing to take emergency action. Fires, loss of electricity, gas leaks, someone drowning in a pool, or a person becoming seriously hurt or unconscious are examples of disasters which might occur in a house or building. Car or bike accidents are emergencies that can happen on the road. No matter what or where an emergency occurs, you need to remember to stay calm.

Most importantly, you should not panic in an emergency. If you panic or get upset, you won't be able to think straight and listen to any emergency directions given. Panicking and getting upset won't help you in an emergency; in fact, it will probably make the situation worse.

Most emergencies are rare and almost never happen, which is why people become scared, upset and panicked when there is an emergency. No matter what the emergency might be, it's always important to be prepared for them, to the best of your ability, if they happen. And most importantly, you need to stay calm!

If you are by yourself and an emergency happens, stay calm and think about what you need to do. Call 911 if you can, and calmly explain the emergency over the phone. Be sure to give your name, your location and as much information as you can about the emergency to the person answering your 911 call.

If you are with others and an emergency happens, stay calm and listen to instructions, such as how to evacuate, and calmly but quickly follow those instructions. Even if people around you are panicking and screaming, make yourself stay as calm and as focused as possible.

Remember, in any emergency, getting panicked and upset won't help you. When you are calm and focused in an emergency, you will be able to listen to instructions and think clearly about what you need to do. Staying calm and focused will help keep you and others safe.

Unit 4: Relationships

Introduction To Relationships

Who Is a Friend?

Meeting New People

Finding and Keeping Friends

Having a Best Friend

Having a Roommate

Employers and Co-workers

Dealing with People Who Don't Like You

Finding a Girlfriend

Finding a Boyfriend

Having a Loving Relationship

Introduction to Relationships

Contrary to what many neuro-typical people believe, most ASD individuals and those with related disabilities want friends as well as a romantic relationship with a significant other at some point in their lives, usually by the time they are in high school or young adulthood. Many individuals with disabilities, including ASD, become sad and sometimes depressed because they want those close relationships but don't know how to achieve them. And often their attempts at a close relationship fall short.

Navigating and managing relationships can be difficult for all of us, whether we have autism or not. Unfortunately, individuals with autism tend to begin actively socializing and looking for relationships much later than their neuro-typical peers. Most people who aren't on the autism spectrum have been honing their social skills from the time they were in preschool. When you are five-years-old, usually all it takes to become friends is to ask someone, "Will you be my friend?" By the time students with ASD reach high school and are actively looking for friends, the rules have changed, and it's no longer that easy to make friends.

By the time neuro-typical teens are in high school, they have had lots of experience with social interactions and various relationships. By contrast, a boy or girl on the autism spectrum might not be ready or even think about forming relationships with their peers until they are in their teens. Regardless of the inherent social and communication difficulties for people with ASD, teens on the spectrum who are trying to form friendships, perhaps for the first time, are already at a distinct disadvantage.

It's important for everyone to have friends. And like everyone else, our children and students with ASD want and need to have friends. Not only do friends help to give us a sense of identity, but when we are with friends we have a group to belong to, and people who will support us, enjoy being with us, and help us feel good about ourselves. Needless to say, we don't want our kids to get involved with people who will take advantage of them, hurt them, or bully them. As most of us know, our kids can be easily duped by people claiming to be their friend. No doubt, many of us know examples of individuals with ASD being manipulated and taken advantage of by people claiming to be their friend. Like many safety lessons, we need to help our teens and adults with ASD learn how to choose their friends wisely.

Finding a boyfriend or girlfriend may be even harder than finding friends for individuals with autism. Their motives are usually good, but how they go about finding and forming a loving relationship with someone is typically "off," immature and, in many cases, clueless. Once they form a loving relationship with someone, it may be hard for an individual with ASD to maintain that relationship. Most relationships require good communication skills, especially with your relationship partner, an amount of flexibility, and realistic expectations. All of that can be difficult for someone on the autism spectrum.

Tips for Teachers/Instructors:

- Get teenagers and young adults with ASD in social groups where they can learn about the social environment of high school and practice/role play their social skills.
- Encourage ASD students to join teams, clubs, and organizations at school.
- Set up a buddy system so that ASD students can join a club/organization or team with a friend and have continued support when they join that club, etc.
- Encourage students to attend school events, such as concerts, games, dances, and stage performances.
- Try to find a club or group that is a good fit for a specific student with ASD. For example, if a student likes theater but can't or won't perform on stage, get him/her involved with stage crew, light board, sound system, organizing the prop table, or doing other theater jobs.
- Above all, be sure your students with ASD aren't loners! Get them eating and sitting with peers and joining at least one group or club.

Tips for Parents:

- Find out how your child's day was - ask specific questions about people, places and activities. Ex: Who did you talk to today? What did you talk about? Who did you sit with during lunch? (Many times, children are not interested in answering questions right after they come home from school, especially if they've had a bad day. You may want to wait until they've had a chance to relax for a while first, if this is the case.)
- If you find that a social interaction went wrong for your child, discuss what went wrong and practice a better way to interact for similar situations in the future.
- Find out who your child's friends are and what they are doing together.
- Encourage your child to join clubs, organizations and teams at school and work with school staff to help it happen.
- Encourage your child to attend school events, but don't always insist on attending with him/her. Encourage him/her to go with peers as much as possible, if your child can handle it.
- If you can, find a peer who can act as a social skills trainer and support for your child.

Tips for Teens and Young Adults with ASD:

- You can't make friends unless you meet people. Get out of your house, go to various school or community events and interact with people.
- Real friends are important! Make friends at school or work, not just online friends.
- If you can, find peer friends to go with you to social events. Don't always depend on your parents to go places with you, and don't only go places with your parents.
- Always try to be polite to people who don't like you, and avoid them if necessary. It's not a good idea to show hostility toward someone. You never know when you will need to work with that person.
- If you want to find a boyfriend or girlfriend, look at your peers who you already know and like. Look at people in your clubs and organizations who you know have interests in common with you.
- Remember, it takes time to find boyfriends or girlfriends and form loving relationships with a special partner. If you don't find someone you can love immediately, don't give up! It takes time to find and form loving relationships.

Who Is a Friend?

A real friend is someone who accepts and likes you for who you are. A real friend doesn't try to control you, but tries to encourage you. A real friend likes to talk to you and wants to spend time with you. A real friend will want to hang out with you and listen to you.

A real friend is dependable, and you can typically trust a real friend. A real friend won't offer you advice unless you ask for it. A real friend will congratulate you when you do a good job and support you when times are tough. Real friends will be there for you at times when you are sad or upset.

Most of all, your real friends are fun to be with. You enjoy being with your friends, and your friends enjoy being with you. Friends typically like to do lots of things together. Most friends have things in common and have some of the same interests. Friends can make you laugh and feel comfortable.

It's not only good to have friends, but friends will help keep you happy and healthy. Everybody needs friends! You can have friends at school, at work, in the neighborhood, and in clubs and organizations. You can find friends almost anywhere.

There are all kinds of friends. Almost everyone has one or two best friends as well as groups of friends from various places. There are also occasional friends, those friends who you see and do things with only occasionally. And finally there are those people who you recognize and possibly know, but they aren't your friends. We call those people acquaintances. An acquaintance can be friendly, but you typically don't know an acquaintance very well, and you wouldn't consider one a friend.

If you are on social media, you might have many friends online. If those social media friends don't actually do things with you, then they probably aren't real, true friends. For example, it is common for people to have many friends on Facebook that are not all friends. The people you "friend" on Facebook may be family members, coworkers, casual acquaintances, people who you go to school with and people who you have never even met. Most of your Facebook friends are probably not going to be real, true friends. If you can't count on them to be trustworthy and dependable, then those social media friends are more like acquaintances than friends.

Usually you and your friends will have a lot in common. You might all be in the same grade or have some classes together. You might have grown-up with your friends in the neighborhood, and you and your friends may have known each other a long time.

You may find that you and your friends like the same games, books, TV shows and sports. You and your friend might like all the same things or do just a few things together. You don't have to like and do everything that your friend does.

Most friends like to play together. Friends can play on a sports team together or just play basketball on a playground or in a park. You can play all kinds of video games or board games with a friend. You can ride bikes, skateboards or scooters together. You can play all kinds of games with friends or just hang out and talk.

Friends usually spend a lot of time talking together. You can talk to a friend at school and chat or text with a friend on the phone. A friend will usually give you his or her phone number, and you would be expected to give your friends your phone number. That way, you can call your friends to talk and to set dates and times to meet. You can keep in touch on the phone or through social media.

Sometimes teenage and young adult friends will eat out together or go to a movie, a ballgame or the mall together. You might join a club, organization or team with a friend. There are many things you can do with your friends.

At school, a friend will sit with you and sometimes save you a seat. A friend will walk with you and hang out with you. You know someone is a real friend if he/she wants to be with you often. You would typically feel relaxed and comfortable being with a friend. It's important to remember that a friend doesn't take advantage of you or bully you. A bully is not a friend!

A friend doesn't need to say he/she is your friend. You just know you are friends. Teenagers and young adults don't need to ask people to be their friend. If you enjoy talking and hanging out with someone, and you find you are spending a lot of time with that person, you can assume you are now friends.

You can share secrets with a friend, because a friend is someone you should trust and respect. You can also share special jokes and stories with a friend. If you find your friend isn't keeping your secrets and you can't trust your friend, then perhaps that person is really not a friend at all.

A friend may sometimes tease you, but friends don't steal from you or demand that you give them things, like money. A real friend won't trick you or embarrass you in a mean way. Even if a friend occasionally teases you, a real friend doesn't do it to be mean to you. If a friend teases you and it makes you upset, you can tell your friend how you feel, and your friend will apologize, and they will usually try not to do it again. Friends don't want to make their friends sad or upset. You also need to remember not to be mean to your friends.

A friend doesn't pretend to be your friend only sometimes. Friends usually don't lie to you. Real friends will be honest with you, even when they are mad at you, and you need to remember to be honest with your friends, too.

Most of the time, friends will do nice things for you just because they are your friends. Be sure and do nice things for your friends, because that's what real friends do.

Friends can have disagreements and sometimes argue. A true friend will still want to be your friend, even if you sometimes argue or get mad at each other.

A friend will listen to you, laugh with you, encourage you, and defend you if someone is mean to you. Everyone needs friends. Your friends enjoy being with you, and you enjoy being with your friends.

Meeting New People

If you want to make friends and create lasting relationships with people, you first need to meet people. Meeting new people face-to-face is sometimes the hardest thing you may do.

There are many places and situations in which you can meet new people. Some people you may meet only once and possibly not meet again. You might meet acquaintances and usually only talk to them briefly. You might meet people who have a lot in common with you and may become your friend. You might meet someone new at work, a party or a social event. You might meet someone when you are by yourself or in a group. You may be introduced to someone you don't know by a friend, a co-worker, or a party host.

Usually if there is a formal introduction and the person introducing you uses your name and the name of the person you are newly meeting, it may be necessary to look at the person's face or eyes and shake his/her hand. This is typically true with formal introductions. It would be rude not to shake someone's hand if he/she extends it toward you. A quick shake of the hand and a brief smile and look at the person's face may be necessary. While shaking a person's hand, you can say, "Nice to meet you." Meeting an employer or a new co-worker might require you to shake hands and say something polite.

Most often, introductions are more casual, especially if they happen at a party or social event. In those cases, it may not be necessary to shake hands. Instead you can smile at the person you are meeting and say "Hi, I'm [say your name]," or if someone tells the person you are meeting your name, you can just say, "Hi, how are you?" After your introduction, you can talk briefly or smile and say, "Nice meeting you" and move away to another person or place.

When you meet someone for the first time and you start a conversation, it's important to take turns talking and chat about acceptable and expected topics. You need to listen to what your conversation partner is talking about and make occasional comments on what he/she is saying.

Things to Say or Talk About with Someone New:

- The event you are both attending; for example, "Isn't this a nice party?" "How do you know the host?" "I really like these appetizers, you should try them" and "I love this music."
- The person's job; for example, "What kind of job do you have?" "Where do you work?" "Do you enjoy working for that company?"
- Movies, television or video games; for example, "Do you like playing video games?" "What's your favorite?" "Have you seen any good movies lately?" "What TV shows do you watch?" "I really like to watch [favorite TV show]."
- Classes, homework and teachers (if you are both in high school); for example, "What classes do you have?" "I think we're in the same P.E. class," "I really like the art teacher."
- Sports; for example, "Do you like basketball?" "What's your favorite team? "I'm a [favorite sports team] fan."
- Travel; for example, "Do you like to travel?" "Where have you been recently? "I'd like to see the ocean someday."
- Pets and family; for example, "Do you have any pets? "I'd love to have a dog someday," "Do you have a big family?" "I have a brother and sister, how about you?"
- Upcoming holidays or weekend events; for example, "Are you going to the football game on Friday?" "What do you like to do on Halloween?" "Are you doing anything fun this weekend?"
- Hobbies and special interests; for example, "So, what do you like to do for fun?" "I really like board games and video games." "What games do you like?"

You or the person you are talking to may introduce any of the above acceptable topics. You might talk briefly about a topic or if you and your new conversation partner enjoy talking about any of these topics, you might talk longer. These accepted topics will help you and your conversation partner find things you both have in common. This could lead to a possible friendship and more opportunities to talk.

Remember, when you are speaking to someone you just met or don't know too well, you need to stay on topic and take turns talking. If you are asking questions, allow the person to answer each question before you ask another question. Actively listen to what the person is saying by looking at his/her face and occasionally nodding. Make occasional comments about what they are saying. Keep your answers to questions short, about one to three sentences long. Small talk is called that because the conversation is not very serious or long. This is not the time to talk at length about a topic or subject that you are interested in. For example, even if you may love to talk about railroad stations, the person you are talking with may not have any interest in railroad stations, and he/she may become bored and leave your conversation. Avoid talking about anything that might be offensive to someone, especially with a person you don't know well. Some topics are simply not appropriate for small talk with anyone.

Inappropriate Subjects to Talk About with Someone New:

- Private/personal information
- Politics and religion (people have very strong opinions about these topics and can become easily agitated when talking about them)
- Possibly offensive jokes
- Sexual information
- Personal health problems or illnesses
- Long, detailed information on a topic of personal interest
- Discussing your or someone else's physical appearance or health problems

Even though it may seem stressful, it can be fun and interesting to meet new people. Meeting new people might help you find new friends as well as a potential boyfriend or girlfriend.

Finding and Keeping Friends

Almost everyone wants and needs friends. Friends are actually important for our health. Having friends can help us to be happy and even healthy. Friends help us to live an enjoyable life.

Friends can do many things for us that we need. Friends listen and talk to us, they support and defend us and they make us feel comfortable and relaxed. Good friends share our secrets, and we can typically trust them.

Friends not only hang out with us and do fun things with us, but friends can also help us when things don't go well or when we need them. Friends are important for everyone.

Who can be a friend? Almost anyone can be your friend, but usually your friends should be about your age. This is especially true of good friends. You may know people you like, such as teachers, adults who help you, friends of your parents, much younger children, and older neighbors. You might think of them as your friends, and that's okay. Your good friends, the friends you do the most with, should be your peers and people who are about your age.

You might make friends online; however, if you only know these people online, you probably don't really know them, and they shouldn't be your only friends. Good friends should be real people, about your age, that you hang out with in a variety of places.

Friends are real people who usually have the same interests as you and like to do many of the things you like to do. You can find most of your friends in the places you go most often. Most people meet friends at school, at work, in clubs/organizations, in the neighborhood and in sports. You can find friends in a variety of places, but you need to get out and look for potential friends in all the places you go to.

If you don't go to many places and you spend a lot of time in your home, you won't meet people who could be your friends. You need to join clubs, organizations, sports teams, interest groups and support groups.

Places to Meet New Peers:

- Classes
- Clubs
- Sports teams
- After-school activities
- Support groups
- Special interest groups
- Church
- Volunteer organizations
- Camps
- Chorus/choir
- Band or theater groups
- Your neighborhood
- Workplace and work-related activities

If there is an activity you enjoy, you can make friends by participating in events and activities where other people enjoy those same things. For example, if you have a dog, you might want to take your dog to a local dog park or another event where people bring their dogs. If you enjoy running, you can sign up to run a marathon. If you love a book or a series of books, you might want to go to a book signing at a book store. If there are movies/TV shows/games/particular interests that have conventions, you can go to those conventions and meet many other people who like the same things. At conventions, renaissance fairs and in Live Action Role-Playing groups, you can wear costumes and dress up as a favorite character. If you enjoy board games or trading card games, you can hang out at a local game store and play games with fellow gamers. These are all great ways to meet and make good friendships. Think of things that interest you and look for events and activities that include that interest, because those are great opportunities to make friends!

You might have online friends who you enjoy interacting with in the comfort of your home. In order to find friends who can go with you to places and interact with you face-to-face, you need to join clubs, organizations, and special interest groups and go places where there are other people who have similar interests as you. You need to get out of your home and meet people who can be your friends.

Once you have friends, it's important that you do things together to maintain the friendship. Sometimes friends go out to eat, go to movies or concerts, play video games, attend sports games and other sporting events or just hang out together and talk.

Examples of activities you can do with a friend:

- <u>Talk or hang out together</u>: talk online or on the phone, hang out at school or each other's homes, or hang out at some other local spot, like a park or library
- <u>Go to ball games or watch games on TV</u>
- <u>Play games</u>: video games, board or card games
- <u>Go to movies, plays or concerts</u>: you can go out to see a show or watch a show on TV at a friend's house
- <u>Play sports outside</u>: basketball, baseball, tennis, biking, skateboarding, etc
- <u>Go to the pool or beach</u>: swimming, sunbathing, water sports
- <u>Go to the mall</u>: shop together at the mall or just walk around
- <u>Ride bikes, walk or jog together</u>: You can also join a fitness facility and go there together
- <u>Take up yoga, tai chi or martial arts class together</u>
- <u>Eat out</u>: go to your favorite restaurants – it's always more fun to eat out with a friend
- <u>Bake or cook together</u>: make food you enjoy, try new recipes or take a cooking class together
- <u>Join a team or sign up for a park district class</u>: park districts typically have team sports, exercise classes and special interest classes
- <u>Join a choir or theater group</u>: church choirs, community choirs and theater groups are always looking for people to join them
- <u>Do a project together</u>: build, make or repair something, learn a DIY project
- <u>Join or create a book club with a friend</u>: consider joining an existing book club or start your own book club with your friends. A book club is a great way to get together to chat and discuss a book you all read.

There are many things you can do with friends, but usually not all friends will want to do everything you enjoy doing. Most people do specific things with specific friends. You may have a friend who loves to play and watch basketball or someone you play video games with. You might have friends who always go to the movies with you or go out to eat with you. It's not unusual for you to have different friends for different activities, and many times people base their friendships on the specific activities they do with their friends.

Most friends keep in touch using social media, text or email. Social media is a great way to contact friends and plan times to get together, to share photos, and keep up with what's happening in their lives. Just don't depend on social media as the only way to interact with your friends. It's important to get out and actually do things with your friends.

Once you have friends, it's important to keep in touch with your friends and do things together. If a friend doesn't hear from you for a long time, that friend may assume you are no longer friends with each other. Friendship is a two-way street. Both you and your friend need to take responsibility for your friendship. Keeping in touch and doing things together are included.

It's important to respect your friend's ideas and respect his/her personal belongings and space. Don't take or use anything belonging to your friend without asking permission. That includes ideas, too. If your friend has a great idea, give him/her the credit for that idea.

When it comes to talking and doing things with a friend, remember that it's not all about you. Take turns talking and listening to each other. It's important to congratulate your friends on their successes and compliment them when it's appropriate. Be sure to allow your friends a turn to talk about their interests and accomplishments. Don't monopolize the conversation or insist on topics of your choice when you are talking with your friends.

Like all relationships, problems and arguments happen occasionally with friends. If you have an argument about something, try to stay calm, and avoid saying anything that's insulting or mean to your friend. Most problems can and should be resolved peacefully. If you want your friendship to continue, you need to solve any problem in a friendly and peaceful way. Sometimes you need to compromise with a friend.

Friends are important to everyone! Remember to cherish your friends, especially your good friends, and treat your friends as you would want them to treat you.

Having a Best Friend

We usually have friends in different situations and places. A person might have some friends on a soccer team and other friends in their classroom. Sometimes we have friends we only see at church, on the school bus, in the neighborhood, or at work. Some friends we might only see during the summer or only during the school year. We can have friends in many different places and in different settings.

We might make new friends in new situations. We might have friends for a long time or just a short time. Some friends we only see occasionally, and some friends we see a lot.

Most people have a best friend or a couple best friends, but not all friends are best friends.

A best friend is a special friend who you trust the most and usually talk to the most. A best friend knows more about you than any other friend. A best friend is usually someone you know well and has been your friend for a long time.

Some people might have a best friend forever ("BFF"). Most people change best friends as they get older or move to a new place. Sometimes when our interests and what's important to us change, so do our best friends. Most people have different best friends throughout their life, because everyone changes, and so our friends often change too.

Who is a best friend? A best friend is someone you can share your secrets with, because you know he or she will keep your secrets. When you are happy, proud, upset, angry, or frustrated, you can share all these thoughts and emotions with a best friend. A best friend can sometimes help you with a problem. A best friend will be with you in good times and when things go bad. A best friend will stick up for you and support you when others won't. A best friend will make you laugh. A best friend might have many of the same interests as you, but not always. Above all, a best friend is someone you can trust.

It's important to have a best friend. We usually all need a best friend. A best friend is usually not someone we only know on the Internet. We can talk to friends on the Internet, but a best friend is someone you should see and talk to face-to- face.

Having a Roommate

Some people prefer to live alone, but many single people like to live with one or more roommates.

Sometimes a person will live with a roommate because it costs less to live in an apartment when you have someone to help share the cost of rent and food. Sometimes a person will have a roommate because having someone live with you is less lonely than living alone.

A roommate can be a helper and a friend. A roommate is usually someone who will talk to you, listen to you and keep you company.

A roommate can help you out if you have a problem or need advice. A roommate can be there if you are sick, worried or lonely.

Sometimes a roommate will go places with you, like a restaurant or the movies. A roommate can watch TV with you, hang out with you and maybe even play video-games or do other activities with you.

There are many good reasons for having a roommate. When you live with a roommate, there are rules you need to follow.

1. Respect the personal belongings of your roommate. You don't touch or take things that belong to your roommate unless your roommate gives you permission. You must ask first before you touch or take things, and if your roommate says no, then you don't touch or take his/her things. That rule also applies to your roommate. Your roommate needs to respect your personal belongings as well.

2. Everyone needs privacy sometimes, and sometimes a roommate wants privacy. A bedroom and a bathroom are private places. Don't go into someone's bedroom or bathroom without knocking. If the door is shut to a bedroom or bathroom, that usually means the person wants privacy.

3. A roommate might not want to talk to you or be with you all the time. Sometimes a roommate needs to be alone in his or her own room. Sometimes roommates want to do things by themselves. You can't assume that a roommate wants to do everything with you. Remember that sometimes you will want to be alone in your room and not bothered by your roommate. Everyone should allow others their alone time.

4. Sometimes a roommate will want to be with other friends, his/her family or co-workers without you. That's okay. Everyone has other people they like to spend time with, including your roommate. You should expect that your roommate will want to do things with other people, besides only you. Don't feel hurt or angry if your roommate sometimes decides to go to an event with a family member, boyfriend/girlfriend or another friend without you.

5. <u>Divide the housework with your roommate, and do your part to keep your house or apartment clean and tidy</u>. You may want to take turns cleaning areas in the apartment or house that you share, like the bathroom, living room and kitchen. You may decide with your roommate to take turns making meals and grocery shopping. There are many things you will need to share responsibility for with your roommate. You need to discuss all these responsibilities with him/her and decide together what you will each do. Neither you nor your roommate should make these decisions alone. Having a roommate means making decisions about your apartment or house together.

6. <u>Living with someone else can sometimes cause arguments about money, food and privacy</u>. If you ever have a disagreement with your roommate, you need to be as polite and calm as possible. You shouldn't yell and fight with others, including your roommate, or soon you won't have a roommate! Figure out what the problem is, and fix it with your roommate.

Sometimes, no matter how hard you try, it may be very hard to live with a roommate. You can't get along with everyone, and sometimes you may need to get a different roommate.

Even if someone doesn't work out as your roommate, you can look for a different person to live with until you find a good match for you. If you really want or need a roommate, you will eventually find the right person to live with.

Employers and Co-workers

When you have a job, you will most likely need to talk and work with an employer, who is your boss, as well as other people, who are your co-workers. Your relationship with a boss and co-workers may be different from other relationships you have. Bosses and co-workers are not necessarily your friends, although some co-workers might become your friends.

An employer, or boss, is typically responsible for hiring you and monitoring your work. A boss may be responsible for training you for the job and evaluating your work progress. A boss may decide how much money you will get for your job and whether you deserve a raise. Remember, a boss wants to be sure you are doing a job correctly and efficiently. A boss is also responsible for firing anyone who is not doing a job well. Depending on where you work, you may have more than one boss. If that's the case, find out what each boss is responsible for regarding your work. Treat all your bosses respectfully, with appropriate and polite behavior.

Sometimes your boss can also be your friend, but don't assume that. Most of the time you will need to treat your boss like a teacher. Pay attention to what your boss tells you, and do your job according to what your boss wants. It's a good idea to be friendly with your boss, but also remember that he/she is in charge, and your boss can fire you if you don't do the job you were hired for. Try not to be too familiar and overly comfortable with your boss, as if your boss was a family member or a friend; your boss might not like that. Treat your boss with friendly respect, but don't forget that your boss is in charge.

Depending on where you work, you may have plenty of time to talk and work with your co-workers. Your co-workers may become your good friends, and when you aren't working, you might have the opportunity to go places and do fun things with your co-workers. Many people develop good friendships with their co-workers.

Sometimes, however, you might have a job in which you don't have an opportunity to get to know your co-workers well. In some jobs, co-workers compete for raises and better job positions, and they might not want to become friends with you for that reason. If you do a very good job and your boss thinks you are great, some co-workers may even become jealous of you.

Occasionally, you may find a co-worker who is a bully. Sometimes a co-worker or boss may act like a bully to make themselves look good and make you look bad. Bullies in the workplace are often insecure about how they are doing their job. A bully at work might make you look like you are doing a bad job so that everyone else will think the bully is doing a great job. That's typically the situation with workplace bullies.

It is best to avoid bullies as much as possible and to continue to do your job well. Bullies aren't typically liked by most people, so you should find other co-workers who don't like the bully and make friends with them. Your new friends can help support you against the bully. Be sure and document your good work as well as any instances the bully disrupts your work or does something inappropriate to you. Write it all down and save the details regarding the bullying against you, since that will be evidence you can present to your boss to show that the bully has done something wrong or is at fault.

It's sometimes difficult to understand the relationships of employers and co-workers. It is usually best to be polite and friendly to everyone, even if you think some of your bosses or co-workers aren't too friendly with you. If you continue to do your job well and are friendly and polite with your bosses and co-workers, you will eventually be respected and liked at your job.

Dealing with People Who Don't Like You

Not everyone will want to be your friend, and not everyone will be nice to you. We all have people we don't like and people who don't like us. Usually, we just avoid the people we don't like or who don't like us. If it's someone we work with or someone we see a lot at school, it might be hard to avoid them.

You may know people you don't like. Whether you don't like someone or someone doesn't like you, you still need to try to be polite. Try not to bother or annoy other people or make anyone mad at you. Think before you speak, and don't say anything hurtful or rude. If you are pleasant and polite to everyone, you will get along with people better and maybe even make new friends.

If you know that something you do annoys someone, try not to act out that behavior when you are with that person. If you don't know what you do that annoys someone, ask a trusted friend to help you figure it out.

If a Person Doesn't Like You:

1. Do you know for sure if someone doesn't like you? What is someone doing which tells you that he/she doesn't like you?
2. Think about what you might be doing which annoys or angers that person.
3. If you don't know what annoys a person, ask a friend to help you figure it out.
4. If necessary, you can say something to that person when no one else is around: For example, "I noticed you frown every time I speak, am I annoying you somehow?"
5. If a person gets angry with you about something you said or did, apologize and tell him/her you didn't mean to annoy or anger him/her. Tell that person you will try not to upset him/her in the future.
6. Continue to be polite and pleasant with someone who doesn't like you. You don't have to be too friendly or apologize constantly.
7. If someone clearly doesn't like you, give him/her space, and try not to bother him/her.
8. Don't force yourself on someone who doesn't like you. You can't force someone to be your friend, and sometimes trying too hard to be friends will annoy a person even more.
9. Don't antagonize anyone, and don't gossip or say bad things about someone who doesn't like you. That will probably make matters worse and might cause any mutual friends to have to pick sides.
10. Continue to be polite and pleasant without overdoing it, and once people get to know you better, they might decide they like you after all.

It's impossible to be everyone's friend, and sometimes it's hard to get along with everyone. This is true of everybody. If someone doesn't like you and you don't know why, just accept it, but continue to be polite to that person anyway. Sometimes a person who doesn't like you at first will like you after they get to know you better.

Don't worry about not being liked by everyone. Nobody is liked by everyone. Instead, concentrate on the friends you do have. Continue to enjoy and be good to the people who do like you, and avoid those who don't like you.

Finding a Girlfriend

Usually when boys are in high school or become young adults, they may want to have a girlfriend. Many young adult men have relationships with a special young lady they call their girlfriend. If an adult man doesn't have a relationship with a girlfriend, they might often be looking for a girlfriend.

Finding girls you might want as a girlfriend is usually easy. You might see girls at school or work who are nice and friendly and who look attractive to you, but having a girl agree to be your girlfriend might be difficult.

Not all girls want to be your girlfriend. Even someone you like very much who you would like to have as your girlfriend may not want to have you as a boyfriend.

No matter how hard you try and no matter how convinced you are that someone would be your perfect girlfriend, if that young woman doesn't want to be your girlfriend, she is not your girlfriend. You cannot make someone be your girlfriend if she doesn't want to be.

You should not give up! There is a girl somewhere who will want to be your girlfriend. You need to keep looking and trying until you find that special girl.

It may be important to you to find a girl who seems nice and good-looking, but it is also just as important to find a special girl who likes you and enjoys many of the things you enjoy.

Instead of approaching girls that you see but don't know, it is usually better to think about someone you already know and are comfortable with as a possible girlfriend.

If you are looking for girls who can be your friend as well as a potential girlfriend, here are some places you might look:

Places to Meet Girls or a Girlfriend:

- Classes
- Clubs
- Sports teams
- After-school activities
- Support groups
- Special interest groups
- Church
- Volunteer organizations
- Camps
- Chorus/choir
- Band or theater groups
- Your neighborhood
- Workplace and work-related activities

Join groups, clubs and organizations that you have an interest in, and look for potential girlfriends in those groups.

It's important to get to know a girl before you ask her to go on a date. It's also important to remember that some girls might like you as a friend, but don't want to be your girlfriend.

When you spend time talking with a girl and getting to know all about her, you can usually figure out if she has the same feelings for you that you have for her. You can have girls who are just friends, and you can have a girlfriend. Girls who are friends and girls who are girlfriends offer very different relationships. You need to recognize when a girl you know likes you only as a friend but not as a girlfriend. Likewise, you need to know the signs a girl may give you that tells you she likes you as a boyfriend and wants to be your girlfriend.

Look carefully at the two charts to understand the differences between a girl who is a friend and a girl who considers herself your girlfriend. You may decide that you only want a girl as a friend, not as a girlfriend.

Is She a Friend or Girlfriend?:

A Girl Who Is Just a Friend:

- She is friendly and nice to me
- She likes to hang out with me
- She talks to me when she sees me
- She might call or text me about school or friends we know
- She usually hangs out with me in a group
- She likes to help me
- If she hasn't seen me in a while she might ask how I'm doing, or say she missed me.
- She likes to sit with me, but not too close
- She doesn't like me to hold her hand, touch her, or kiss her
- She won't go on a date with me by herself
- She doesn't tell anyone she's my girlfriend or she wants to be my girlfriend

A Girl Who Is a Girlfriend:

- She will call, text and email me a lot, just to talk to me
- She will agree to go on dates, just the two of us
- She likes to sit close to me and touch me
- She may tell me she misses me if she doesn't hear from me or see me almost everyday
- She's happy to see me
- She likes to be alone with me
- She will hug me and likes it when I hold her hand, touch her back, and maybe kiss her
- She will tell her friends that I'm her boyfriend or she wants me to be her boyfriend
- She may expect me to take her to dances and special events
- She will tell me she likes me a lot or even loves me
- She might give me cards and little presents

The best way to get to know a girl is to talk to her and spend time with her. If you enjoy each other's company and like being together, you might ask her on a date.

When you go on a date, you do special things together. Maybe you will go to a movie or to a restaurant together. You could go on a bike ride, to a ball game, or just walk around the mall together. When you ask someone on a date, you are telling her that you like her and want to spend time alone with her. Asking a girl on a date means you would like to think of her as a girlfriend instead of just as a friend.

When it comes to dating, you need to take things slowly to see if you might want to do more things together. Give yourself time to get to know each other and become comfortable with each other. Perhaps after a few dates, if you both decide you really like each other, you might move toward a more intimate relationship, such as holding hands and kissing.

A guy would typically not ask a girl, "Do you want to be my girlfriend?" Instead, after a few dates, it may be understood between you and this one girl that you are dating and therefore are boyfriend and girlfriend.

It is always best to have a girlfriend you can interact with face-to-face. You may be comfortable and happy to have an online-only girlfriend. An online girlfriend is perfectly fine, as long as you accept the fact that your girlfriend might not be truthful about herself. Remember that if you have an online girlfriend, you need to be careful not to be taken advantage of. Don't give an online girlfriend any money, credit card information or personal information about yourself, such as your social security number.

Sometimes a boyfriend/girlfriend relationship may eventually lead to a more intimate, sexual relationship. Just remember, sex should only be for adults, and it must always be consensual, which means that every time you have any type of sex, both you and your partner (boyfriend/girlfriend) must agree to it. Also, you need to be responsible for safe sex each and every time you have sex with anyone.

Suggested Girlfriend Rules:

1. You should accept your girlfriend for who she is and not want or attempt to change her. Your girlfriend should also accept you for who you are.
2. You and your girlfriend should enjoy being with each other and talking together. Your girlfriend also needs to be your friend.
3. Both you and your girlfriend should be kind to and considerate of each other.
4. You need to respect your girlfriend and accept her personal decisions.
5. You shouldn't push your girlfriend to be more intimate with you if she isn't comfortable with it. Your girlfriend shouldn't push you for intimacy if it makes you uncomfortable.
6. Do not demand sex from your girlfriend! Demanding sex or insisting on doing anything that your girlfriend is uncomfortable with is wrong and possibly unlawful!
7. Even though you may have occasional arguments with your girlfriend, it is not acceptable for either of you to be verbally, mentally and emotionally abusive with each other. If your relationship becomes verbally and emotionally abusive, you need to end it!
8. Physical abuse, such as hitting, biting, kicking and otherwise purposefully harming each other, is not acceptable, and if that ever happens, you should end the relationship immediately!

You may find a girlfriend who will be your girlfriend for a long time or just a short time. Most people date several people before they find the special person who will be a longtime girlfriend. Don't give up looking for a girlfriend. Somewhere there is a special girlfriend for you.

Finding a Boyfriend

When most girls become teenagers, they begin to think more about boys and having a boyfriend. This may start as early as junior high or even elementary school. Having a boyfriend becomes important for many girls. Teenage girls may talk about how cute a boy is and might do things to get noticed by boys. Girls will wear cute, fashionable clothes and worry about how they look. Girls will often spend a lot of time on their hair and makeup in order to look their best.

For some girls, it may be important to be part of a group of friends so that boys will think they are popular and want to date them. Girls might compete for the attention of boys and look for possible boyfriends.

You might see many boys who you think are cute and you'd like to date. Know that popular, cute boys might not be good potential boyfriends for you. It's better to find boys who have more in common with you and who like the same things as you. A boyfriend needs to first be a friend – someone who enjoys talking to you and perhaps has the same hobbies and interests as you.

When it comes to finding a boyfriend, think about the boys you already know and see in classes, clubs or teams. Think about the boys you enjoy talking to and are comfortable with. Look for boys who like you for who you are.

Places to Meet Boys or a Boyfriend:

- Classes
- Clubs
- Sports teams
- After school activities
- Support groups
- Special interest groups
- Church
- Volunteer organizations
- Camps
- Chorus/choir
- Band or theater groups
- Your neighborhood
- Workplace and work-related activities

Join groups, clubs and organizations that you have an interest in, and look for potential boyfriends in those groups.

It is always best to have a boyfriend you can interact with face-to-face. You may be comfortable and happy with an online-only boyfriend. An online boyfriend is perfectly fine, as long as you accept the fact that your boyfriend might not be truthful about himself. Remember that if you have an online boyfriend, you need to be careful not to be taken advantage of. Don't give an online boyfriend any money, credit card information or personal information about yourself, such as your social security number.

Once you have a boyfriend, you will want to think about your relationship and decide together how intimate you want to be with each other. Maybe you are uncomfortable with the idea of intimacy or are not ready to be intimate with a boyfriend yet. For example, you may be fine with holding hands with a boyfriend and occasionally kissing, but sexual touching and engaging in sex is too uncomfortable or not appropriate. When it comes to intimacy with a boyfriend, only do what you are comfortable doing.

Having sex with your boyfriend is a big decision, and probably one you shouldn't make until you are both adults. Having a boyfriend doesn't mean you need to be intimate or have sex. In fact, you should never have sex until you are over the age of consent, able to be responsible for your actions, and you are sure having sex is what you want to do.

Anyone who is abusive, demanding or insists on having sex with you in order to be your boyfriend is NOT a good boyfriend, and you need to stop seeing that person immediately!

Suggested Boyfriend Rules:

1. Your boyfriend should accept you for who you are and not want or attempt to change you.
2. You and your boyfriend should enjoy being with each other and talking together. Your boyfriend needs to also be your friend.
3. Both you and your boyfriend should be kind and considerate with each other.
4. Your boyfriend should respect you and accept your personal decisions.
5. Your boyfriend shouldn't push you to be more intimate with him if you aren't comfortable doing so.
6. You need to end your relationship and "break up" if your boyfriend tells you that he won't be your boyfriend unless you have sex with him.
7. Even though you may have occasional arguments with your boyfriend, it is not acceptable for either of you to be verbally, mentally and emotionally abusive with each other. If your relationship becomes verbally and emotionally abusive, end it!
8. Physical abuse, such as hitting, biting, kicking and otherwise purposefully harming each other, is not acceptable, and if that ever happens, you should end the relationship immediately!

You may find a boyfriend who will be your boyfriend for a long time, or just a short time. Most people date several people before they find a special person who will be a longtime boyfriend. Don't give up looking for a boyfriend. Somewhere there is a special boyfriend for you who will like you for who you are.

Having a Loving Relationship

Many people dream of finding a special someone to have a lasting and loving relationship with, and someday maybe even getting married. Most people want a loving partner or spouse who they can live with and share their lives with. This is the hope of many adults, but finding that special someone can be hard.

You can date a lot of people and like a lot of people, but loving someone takes a deeper and more mature or serious commitment. Saying, "I love you" to a boyfriend or girlfriend is a big and sometimes risky step to take in a relationship.

Usually when you say, "I love you" to someone, you are hoping and expecting that he/she will have the same feelings for you and will say "I love you" back. If you discover that you both love each other very much, then you and your boyfriend/girlfriend may be on your way to becoming a committed and loving couple. And if you love each other and want to share a life together, you may decide to get engaged to be married someday, or perhaps share a home together until you know for sure that marriage is for you.

Sharing a home together and even planning on getting married is an important step and is not something you should decide on without a lot of thought or too quickly. It takes being an adult and knowing what you want in life, as well as what you want in a partner or spouse before you can commit to a serious, long-term relationship.

If you have a boyfriend/girlfriend and the two of you have been a couple for at least a year and you love each other, it's always a good idea to discuss your long-term plans together. Don't assume you both have the same ideas and plans. This is why people usually date each other for a while, often a year or more, and get to know each other really well before deciding that they found the one person they love enough with which to make a long-term, marriage-type commitment.

Questions to Ask Yourself and Partner Before Living Together:

- Are you both adults?
- Are you both able to live independently?
- Are you both compatible and able to live together?
- Do you both have the same idea about your relationship? For example, do you both want to get married someday?
- Are you both able to work and keep a job?
- What will you do if one of you loses his/her job?
- Do you both drive?
- Do you know each other well, and are you okay with each other's habits?
- Are you both able to communicate your thoughts and feelings with each other?
- Are you able to compromise with each other's routines, tastes in food, music and leisure activities?
- Do you both like or want pets?
- Do you like each other's friends and family members?
- How will you divide payment for rent, food, utilities and other expenses?
- How will you divide household chores?

Questions to Ask Yourself and Partner Before Getting Married:

- Are you able to get married, and will your families support the idea of your marriage?
- Where will you live?
- Will you both work?
- Will you have enough money to live together as a married couple?
- Do you both want children?
- How will you handle any differences in religion?
- Do you have the same ideas about what's most important in life?
- Can you agree on what to spend your money on and how much you need to save?
- If you have separate checking or savings accounts, how will you decide together who pays for what?
- Will you consider your spouse's opinion before making plans or decisions; for example, making a big purchase, taking a trip, inviting people over, and buying something you both will use?
- Are you in agreement about sex and your sexual activities?
- Are you able to argue constructively without hurting each other's feelings?
- Are you committed to loving each other and working out any problems, no matter how hard a problem may be?

When you find that special person who you love and want a long-term commitment with, that is only the beginning. There are many things you need to consider before committing to a loving relationship. Being married, or being in a long-term and loving relationship, means that you and your spouse or partner need to work hard to keep your relationship healthy and long lasting.

Most importantly, if you are in a loving relationship, you need to communicate well together. No relationship will last unless you are both able to talk about your feelings and thoughts, especially about things that are important to both of you. Remember that communication is a two-way street. You both need to talk to each other and listen to each other. When you make decisions or plans, discuss it with your partner before acting on it, especially if those plans or decisions involve your partner. Don't assume your partner can read your mind, just like you can't read his/her mind. Make it a point to talk to you partner every day about a variety of topics, not just the ones you want to talk about.

Treat your partner with kindness, consideration, and respect. If you don't treat each other with respect, your relationship probably won't last. Be open and honest with your partner. If either of you are lying and/or being deceitful, your relationship will eventually end. Try not to take your partner for granted, and remember to treat your partner the way you would like your partner to treat you.

Sometimes relationships don't work out, no matter what you do. Sometimes a loving relationship will break up, or a marriage will end in divorce. Those kinds of break-ups are very hard on a couple as well as on your family and friends. Because of that, it's important that you think carefully about all the questions you and your partner need to consider before you begin a long-term relationship as a couple.

If you can't find that special person for a loving relationship as soon as you'd like, or if you can't seem to stay in a long-term relationship with someone you love, don't give up! It takes time and sometimes many tries before you find someone who you can love, and who will love you for who you are.

Unit 5: Personal Safety

Introduction to Personal Safety

Personal safety is defined here as safety for your own well-being and keeping yourself safe when there is danger from others. There are many ways to stay safe in various environments with things we use or come in contact with. Sometimes our safety is compromised by people who may wish us harm. This section addresses personal safety when we face potential harm from others.

Most of us know that individuals with disabilities, including Autism Spectrum Disorder (ASD), are at risk of being taken advantage of or harmed, as well as being sexually molested and abused. According to the Disabilities Information Center, one in five children with ASD have been physically abused, and one in six children with ASD have been sexually abused. According to a recent survey of adults with ASD in Canada, it is estimated that 78 percent of teens and young adults on the autism spectrum are victims of sexual abuse, sexual coercion and rape (Ben Wolford).

Because of their vulnerability, naivety and often inability to solve social problems, it's important that we teach them about their personal safety and prepare them to the best of their ability to handle these difficult and sometimes traumatic situations.

There may come a time when even a child with ASD is old enough and capable of being home alone. A teenager who is home alone may understand specific safety rules within the house, but dealing with strangers who come to the door or call on the phone is another matter. Since many individuals with autism are easily deceived or persuaded to do what others tell them, a stranger could take advantage of a situation when a teenager or young adult with ASD is home alone. Being home alone requires knowing how to handle strangers or even acquaintances who come to the door or call on the phone.

The realities of ASD individuals being targeted by bullies are more apparent and frequently documented. Bullying individuals with ASD is also becoming epidemic, especially as students are typically mainstreamed into the general school population without adult supervision or assistance. Kids with autism are easy targets for abuse because they are often naïve, and they usually don't have a support group of friends. ASD teens are easily scared, and they typically have a hard time understanding and problem-solving difficult situations. Unfortunately, most teens with autism have been bullied, and some even severely. Bullying is a huge problem among those in the ASD population. As parents, teachers, therapists and employers, we need to assume that bullying is happening and be vigilant about it. As a precaution, we need to educate teens and young adults with ASD on how to handle any occurrences of bullying. Furthermore, we need to take any reports of bullying seriously and act on them. We shouldn't dismiss it when our kids report any incidence of bullying or tell them to just ignore it.

Many individuals with autism enjoy using the computer and other social media devices. They typically feel more comfortable talking to others online, rather than in person. Many of them are very good at navigating the Internet. They enjoy interacting with people in online communities and exploring various topics of interest online. Unfortunately, with the increased dangers of scams, computer viruses, online stalkers, pedophiles, cyberbullying, and access to questionable and inappropriate internet sites, the computer and other social media devices become another source of potential danger for children, teens and young adults with ASD. As parents of kids with ASD, we need to pay attention to what our kids are doing online and guard against any illegal or potentially dangerous activities that they may be engaged in. Everyone should be involved in educating teens and young adults about online and social media dangers.

The rules of appropriate and inappropriate touching become complicated as teens and young adults start exploring a variety of relationships. Understanding the boundaries and parameters of touching becomes increasingly more important as kids grow older and start to develop relationships as well as interact with a larger and more diverse group of people. With children, the rules of touching can be explained in black-and-white terms. For older teens and adults, those rules become more gray and situation specific. The rules of touching may become stricter in some situations, yet looser and almost nonexistent in others. Nonetheless, the topic of appropriate and inappropriate touching should be reviewed and discussed with teens and young adults. We can't assume that these individuals with ASD will automatically understand and apply the changing rules of touching to specific people and situations.

Likewise, as individuals with ASD become more independent and begin going to places and doing things on their own, they need to understand potentially dangerous situations and know what to do when people cause them or intend to bring them harm. We may want to protect them from the knowledge of such dangers, but in actuality, the more they know about what to expect and the more prepared they are, the less anxious they should be.

Rape is not a subject we ordinarily think about or choose to discuss with our children and students. Yet, given the sexual abuse statistics of people with disabilities, it may be a necessary topic to teach for the safety of adolescents and young adults with ASD. Since people with disabilities are easily taken advantage of, they need to understand the difference between consensual sex and rape. Furthermore, no one should EVER be bullied or forced into sex. You always have the choice to say 'No' and run away or fight, if necessary. It is also important that individuals understand they must seek immediate help if they are sexually assaulted or raped. This section offers two chapters on rape. One is written more simply, and can be used as a possible introduction to this difficult topic. The other chapter discusses rape in depth and answers a number of questions individuals with ASD might have about it.

Tips for Teachers/Instructors:

- Assume that students with ASD are being bullied, and be vigilant monitoring any unsupervised places, such as bathrooms, locker rooms, parking lots.
- Let all students with ASD know how to respond to and report any bullying that happens to them at school or on social media from other students.
- Remind students of the rules and consequences of fighting or bringing weapons to school.
- Give students a safe, trustworthy adult who they can turn to when they are faced with scary and difficult situations at school.
- Educate students on abuse, molestation, rape and online bullying.

Tips for Parents:

- Always ask about your child's day. Ask him/her specific questions about people, places and activities. Look for indications of bullying or someone taking advantage of your child.
- Talk to your child about bullying, abuse, molestation and rape in such a way as to make him/her understand what they need to do, without making them feel overly scared or anxious about those potential problems. Help them feel confident in their knowledge of these dangers.
- Tell your children to immediately tell you if anyone threatens or abuses them, even if the abuser threatens them with harm if they talk to you. Contact the school and/or police if your child has been threatened or harmed. Don't be reluctant to take action on behalf of your child!
- Make sure your child has a cell phone (and knows how to make calls on it) or get your child a GPS tracker or similar device if you are concerned about finding your child when he/she is somewhere on his/her own.
- Pay attention to what your children are doing online. Even if your child becomes better at navigating online than you, you need to keep tabs on what they are doing and educate them about scams and social media hazards.

Tips for Teens and Young Adults with ASD:

- Don't hide or keep incidents of bullying or abuse to yourself. Always talk to parents, trusted adults and even friends if you are dealing with a scary and difficult problem which might be, or definitely is, harmful to you.
- No relationship is worth saving if it is abusive. If a friend, boyfriend or girlfriend is abusing you mentally, physically or emotionally, you need to end that relationship.
- Being independent is great, but beware of situations which put you in potential danger. If you are going anywhere alone, tell trusted friends and adults where you are going and what you are doing. Bring a phone with you, and contact police or trusted friends/family if you have a problem. It's always better to be safe.
- You may have great computer skills and feel very comfortable doing many things online and on social media. Understand that everything you do online leaves a history and can be traced. Be sure you don't do anything that's illegal or that may compromise your safety.

Strangers on the Phone or at the Door

Strangers might call on the phone or come to the door of your home and knock or ring the doorbell. Usually these people aren't dangerous, and we don't need to worry about them. If we don't know them and we don't know what they really want, it's always best to avoid these strangers.

If the phone rings and you don't recognize the number, it's usually a good idea not to answer it. If the call is important, the person calling will leave a message. Usually, if a stranger calls, he/she is trying to sell you something or is asking for a money donation.

If you do answer the phone and it's someone you don't know, don't tell that person anything about you or your family or any personal information, including your address. Don't promise to give that person any money, and don't agree to buy anything this person is trying to sell you. Don't give that person any credit or debit card numbers, social security numbers or banking information. When they try to sell you something or ask for money, just say, "No thank you" and hang up the phone. You might have to hang up the phone while the stranger is still talking to you, and that's okay.

If the person on the phone asks to talk to a parent, don't tell that person that you are home alone, even if it's true. Tell him or her that your parent "is busy right now." Ask the person on the phone if you can take a message, and then ask the person for his or her name. If the stranger on the phone asks if anyone is home with you or if you are home alone, don't tell them you are alone. You can tell the stranger on the phone that someone is with you, or that you expect a family member to arrive home soon. This might be a lie, but it is a necessary lie to keep you safe.

Sometimes if you're home alone, someone you don't know may come to the door. Usually people who come to the door aren't dangerous. A person who comes to the door might be there to drop off a package or newspaper, to sell something or to ask for money for a charity. These people might be annoying, but they are usually not dangerous.

You don't know for sure if a stranger at the door is a safe or dangerous person. It's always a good idea to keep the door shut and locked and not let a stranger into the house, especially if you are home alone.

It's not likely, but if a stranger comes into your house, the stranger might try to hurt you. If a stranger knows you are home alone, that stranger might try to steal things in your house. People who steal things – burglars, robbers and thieves – are all criminals, and they can also be dangerous to you and your family.

Sometimes the stranger at the door wants to deliver something. Unless you are expecting a package that day, it's still not a good idea to open the door. Most people who deliver packages will ring the doorbell to let you know you have a package, and then will place the package by your front door and leave. People delivering things to your door will not try to come into your house. They will always stay outside. Often they are in a hurry and will leave right away, because they have many other packages to deliver. Even if a stranger has a package and wants you to open the door, don't do it. He/she can leave the package, leave a note or come back later. Sometimes there are packages that you need to sign for; these are special deliveries, and the delivery company or the company you ordered the item from will let you know beforehand that you will need to sign for the package when you make the purchase. They may also call you the day before to remind you. If someone is at your door with a delivery that they say you need to sign for, but you did not order anything that requires a signature, then you might not want to open the door if you are home alone. That's okay; you don't ever need to open the door to a stranger!

Sometimes the stranger at the door might pretend to be there to fix something. Unless you expect a repairman and that repairman was expected to come at that time, you shouldn't open the door. You don't know if a stranger at the door is telling you the truth, and a stranger might lie to get you to open the door.

If a Stranger Rings Your Phone or Doorbell:

- If the phone rings and you don't recognize the number, it's usually best not to answer it. It will probably be someone wanting to sell you something.
- If you answer the phone and it's someone you don't know, do not tell that person anything about your family, or give any personal information, such as credit card numbers, a social security number or anything else that person asks you for.
- Don't promise to give that person any money. Just say, "No thank you," and hang up the phone.
- Don't let a stranger on the phone know that you are home alone.
- Don't open the door to a stranger.
- If a stranger knocks on your door or rings the doorbell, make sure the door is locked.
- If the stranger continues to ring the doorbell or knocks even when you don't answer the door, call your parents or roommate to see if someone is expected, and find out what you should do.
- It's usually not a good idea to have a conversation with a stranger on the other side of the door. The stranger might try to convince you to open the door. Most people would just ignore the stranger until he/she leaves.

- If the stranger calls to you through the door with an important message, or if there's an emergency, you may decide to answer the stranger, while still keeping the door closed until you know it's safe to open it.
- If the person at your door says he/she is a police officer, but you can't see his/her badge, tell this person you will call 911 to verify his/her identity and the reason for being at your door.
- If you can see the police officer's badge and identity, and you know that it is a police officer, open the door.

There is always a possibility that a stranger might find a way to get into your house anyway. A stranger could go through an unlocked door or window to get into your house. If a stranger finds a way to get into your house, this could be a scary and dangerous situation.

If a stranger or dangerous person sneaks in or breaks into your home while you are there alone, quickly run to a room with your cell phone or where you know there is a phone. Be sure it's a room with a lock, and lock yourself inside. Once locked safely inside the room, immediately call 911 for help. It's not okay to be alone in the house with a stranger.

If the person at the door says he/she is a police officer, but you can't see the police badge, and you have no other way of determining if the stranger is a police officer, tell that person you will call a parent as well as 911. It is best to be cautious. Don't answer the phone if you don't recognize the person calling, and keep the door to your home closed and locked. Don't ever let strangers into your house, especially if you're alone.

The Internet and Social Media

Talking to People Online

Most of us like to use the computer and other devices to access social media. The Internet can be helpful and give us lots of information. We can learn a lot online, and we can comfortably meet people online and on social media sites and apps.

When we go online with our computer or other devices, we need to know about the dangers of talking to strangers through various Internet platforms, such as email, messaging apps, chat rooms, video channels, blogs, online forums and Facebook.

Unless we use video chats/calls, we can't see the people we talk to online, so we don't really know who they are. A person online might say he/she is your age and just like you. The person online might claim to be your friend. Someone you meet online may tell you he/she likes you and wants you as a boyfriend/girlfriend.

It's easy for people we meet online to lie to you. Many people online tell you information you want to hear, but it might not be the truth. Sometimes strangers online will lie to you because they want to gain your trust. They want you to like them and do something for them.

A stranger online might ask for personal information about you or your family. It's important never to give personal information to someone online, especially when that person asks for it. It's usually not a good idea to give money to people who claim to be your friends, but it's especially important to never send money to someone you only know online. Friends are never going to ask you for banking information, credit card numbers or social security numbers, or ask you to give them large amounts of money.

Computer viruses and other malicious or invasive downloads such as malware or adware are a constant danger on the Internet. Be sure you have a good antivirus program installed on your computer and that you keep it up-to-date. An up-to-date antivirus program will detect most viruses on your computer and keep them from destroying or harvesting data from your computer. Don't open attachments from people you don't know, and don't open suspicious emails. Email scams in particular have become very common; they come in the form of an email that is very vague and contains very little text but has an attachment or a link to click on that is often malicious, even if the email appears to come from a friend or family member. If an email has a title or text that says something unspecific and simple, such as, "I thought you would like this!" or "This is so funny! Click this!", you should never click on those links or download those attachments unless you recognize the email address of the person who sent them. You should then reply to that person to make sure that it was really them who sent you the attachment or link, rather than someone else using their email account. If they confirm that they DID send you the link or attachment, then you are probably safe to click on it.

Even people who are very good at recognizing and avoiding potential viruses and malware will periodically get malicious software on their computer. It is nearly impossible to completely avoid! That's why, if you have important data or documents, it's important to back them up and have an up-to-date antivirus program to protect your computer and data.

Talking to Someone Online Rules:

1. Don't believe everything a person tells you online.
2. If someone online asks for private, confidential information, such as your social security number, credit card numbers and other account numbers, don't EVER give them that information.
3. Don't send money to anyone you meet online, even if that person tells you a sad story about needing money. Even if someone online claims to be your boyfriend or girlfriend, you should NOT send them any money.
4. Don't tell someone where you live or give them information about your family.
5. Don't ever go alone to meet someone you talk to online. It is usually never a good idea to meet with someone you talk to online at all, but if you need to, always take a parent or trusted adult with you just in case the person isn't who he/she claims to be.
6. If someone who is not a trusted boyfriend or girlfriend talks about sex with you online, that is wrong. Tell your parents or a trusted adult if someone online is talking about sex with you, sending you sexually provocative photos or verbally engaging in sex with you.
7. It is very common for people online to say offensive and hurtful things to other people who they do not know. It is important to try not to let those hurtful comments bother and upset you
8. If hurtful comments from other people are upsetting you, you can usually block those people or report them. If those actions do not stop someone from harassing you, especially if the person harassing you is someone you know offline, you should tell your parents or guardian, and they might need to tell the school or police.
9. It is very important never to text, message or post anywhere online any photos of yourself naked or in underwear or engaging in any sexual activity.
10. Once you have uploaded a photo, it can be saved and shared by many people, all over the world. It is impossible to prevent an embarrassing photo or video from being seen by anyone once it has been uploaded and sent somewhere. If someone asks for a naked or sexy photo or video, you should simply refuse. It is better to make someone annoyed by not sending them a picture, than to risk being humiliated.
11. Save emails or information someone sends you which is threatening, illegal, false, or makes you uncomfortable. If you or a parent needs to take legal action against that person, those saved records will provide evidence to support you.

12. **Verify any suspicious-looking emails, and never click on links or download attachments before being sure that they aren't malicious. Always back up important data and documents, and have a good and up-to-date antivirus program.**

Insults and harassment are very common online. It is common for people to say insulting things to others while playing online video or computer games, leave rude comments under videos, say rude things about artwork, and insult the way other people look, etc. People tend to feel very brave and bold online, and say things they would not normally say to someone's face, but they find it fun and exciting to say those insulting things when they are online. If someone is saying something that you find hurtful and/or offensive, you can turn off your headset, find a new group of people to play with, turn off comments/chat options, or even have users blocked or banned. Many forums and social media platforms have strict rules against harassment and will take action if you report another user for harassment or offensive behavior.

Most of the time, hurtful things said online are just part of the general online chatter. Even though many comments are rude and inappropriate, often the person making the comment is young and doesn't understand they might really be hurting someone's feelings. They often just think they are making a joke, but it's difficult to tell when someone is making a joke online and when they are being serious. That is why it is often best to ignore those rude comments if possible.

Sometimes, rude comments online become real harassment. Sometimes a person may follow you across many social media platforms, sending mean messages to you, having their friends send mean messages to you, texting you, emailing you and bothering you every time and everywhere you go online. When you aren't able to simply ignore or block someone and have their harassment stop, this is a problem. It's important to take screen caps of messages and save the harassing messages sent to you, as well as to tell your parents or guardians.

If the person harassing or bullying you is someone you know at school, the school will need to be notified. If it's someone else, or you don't know who they are, then the police may need to be called. Often, if the person harassing you is using a certain website, app, game, or social media platform, you can report the user to the site/app. Most sites/apps have easy ways to report other users for harassment.

It's common for people to think that they can say mean things online and not get in trouble because you don't know who they are. The police can find out exactly who they are, and those people who are threatening or harassing you will definitely get in trouble. If you feel like you are being personally harassed online, do not feel scared or embarrassed to take action.

Words and ideas online can be hurtful and threatening. It is usually easier for someone to say hateful things to you online instead of in person. If someone tells you hateful things online and threatens you or tells you to harm yourself, don't get upset, and don't do what the person wants you to do. Instead, save the threatening message, and tell parents, trusted adults and possibly the police.

Writing and Posting Online

You can talk to others online through email, text, direct messages, chat rooms, forums, video games, vlogs, blogs, YouTube, Twitter, Facebook, Tumblr, Snapchat, Reddit, etc.

We might think that only a certain person or a certain group of people will see our message or post, but that might not be true. Information on the internet, even in private messages or posts, can end up being read by many people.

Sometimes parts of our message or post can be cut and pasted and sent to another person without our consent or knowledge. Sometimes the entire message is forwarded or copied and saved or sent to someone else. Pictures we send can easily be saved and re-shared. Even private messages can be screen capped, saved and shared.

We need to remember that whatever we put online is not ever truly confidential. Personal, private information we put online might be read by many people. Personal, private pictures we send online might be seen by many people. Sometimes information we put online can get us in trouble if the wrong person gets that information.

If you tell someone online that you are going to perform a crime or are thinking about doing something violent or illegal, that message or post could get you into serious trouble. For example, if a person says he plans to start a fire at school or work, bring a gun to school or work, or physically harm property or people, just writing that in a message or post could get him suspended, expelled from school or fired from work and possibly arrested.

It does not matter if you are just making a joke or don't mean to do anything you are posting about, because no matter what your intent is, the police will take those statements very seriously, and you will get into trouble, and possibly be arrested. Someone getting an online message from you about a crime might not realize you are joking and will call the police or tell school staff about it.

Criminal Actions on the Internet

As hard as it may seem to understand, some things we read, download or purchase online may be illegal. Even if something we do on our computers isn't illegal, it may be considered a possible criminal action and may be enough to cause the police or FBI to investigate you.

Most people think that what they do online or with their own computer is personal and private, and no one will know about it. That isn't true. Many people can get your personal information from your computer without you even knowing it. And any criminal actions will usually alert the police.

The following list of actions is considered illegal or a possible criminal action and may cause you to be investigated and possibly arrested. Even if you go to various sites out of curiosity and don't have any actual criminal intent, just visiting certain illegal or inappropriate sites could get you arrested or at least cause you to be investigated.

- Buying, selling and using stolen credit cards (credit cards taken without permission) online
- Hacking government, military, corporation or business websites
- Taking money which doesn't belong to you from online accounts
- Asking about purchasing illegal drugs or offering to sell drugs online
- Viewing or searching for websites which show you how to murder someone, build a bomb, or commit other crimes
- Searching for or attempting to join a terrorist organization online
- Viewing, downloading and purchasing child pornography

Even if you are sitting at your computer in the privacy of your own home or your parents' home, if you do any of the criminal actions from this list, you will very likely be investigated and possibly arrested. There are many places on the internet where people are involved in illegal activities – these areas are full of not only criminals, but also federal agents and other investigators who are there to catch criminals. It is not a good idea to even be curious about the websites that talk about illegal activities, because then the police might think that YOU are a criminal, too.

The police will come to your door, search your house, take your computer and take you in for questioning. If the police find you are guilty of doing illegal things on your computer, they may arrest you.

A computer is a wonderful device for meeting people and gathering information. It's important to remember that everything we do online and in social media is never private. All the sites we go to and all the people we meet and interact with online, and through any social media can be viewed by many others.

Dealing with Verbal and Emotional Abuse

People can hurt us with what they say and do, even if they don't physically harm us. Sometimes what someone says to us can make us feel bad about ourselves. The words and actions of others can make us feel sad, anxious and scared.

Sometimes verbal and mental/emotional abuse can feel worse than being hit and physically hurt by someone. When someone says or does something mean or degrading in order to purposely make you feel bad about yourself and cause you to feel anxious, depressed or scared, that is verbal and emotional abuse.

Sometimes people can take advantage of you because they think it would be easy to manipulate you and convince you of something. If you think someone is taking advantage of you or making you say, do or think anything that makes you feel uncomfortable, bad or afraid, you need to tell a parent or trusted adult.

Most often, verbal and emotional abuse is something you might expect from bullies and people who aren't your friends or who dislike you. Anyone can say or do something that would make you feel sad or scared. Sometimes even people you love can say or do mean and horrible things, which make you feel bad about yourself.

Emotional abuse can often last a long time and can get worse as time goes on. Emotional and mental abuse can make you feel worthless, helpless and at fault or guilty for many things, even if you haven't done anything wrong. If you are abused for a long time, you might think that it's a normal and acceptable part of your life. You may not feel a need to end the emotionally abusive relationship with your friend, boyfriend/girlfriend, spouse, or co-worker. If you experience verbal and emotional abuse, even for a short time, you will probably feel anxious, helpless and depressed. You may have a hard time learning, working or doing the things you enjoy. Sometimes verbal and emotional abuse can lead to physical abuse.

Verbal and emotional abuse isn't good for anyone! You need to recognize those behaviors which are considered verbal, emotional, mental and psychological abuse. Here are some examples of this abuse:

- Repeatedly and intentionally embarrassing you
- Severely and repeatedly insulting you
- Intentionally telling you things that make you anxious or scared
- Controlling you by telling you what to do, even if you don't want to do it, or telling you to do something that makes you feel uncomfortable and bad
- Threatening to harm you
- Threatening to expose your secrets or spread mean rumors about you
- Telling you that you are worthless, useless, stupid, and that no one likes you
- Stalking you

If you are in an intimate relationship with someone, the signs of verbal and emotional abuse might include the following (yourtango.com, 2016, "21 Signs You're in an Emotionally Abusive Relationship" by Marni Feuerman):

- Threatening to physically hurt you, your family or a pet
- Getting angry or making you feel bad if you don't consent to sexual activity
- Purposely ignoring you or refusing to communicate with you
- Keeping you away from your friends and family
- Demonstrating extreme jealousy for no apparent reason
- Being very dominating and controlling of you
- Blaming you for everything or making everything your fault
- Threatening to commit suicide if you leave

If someone is verbally and emotionally abusing you, you need to end or leave that relationship. Verbal and emotional abuse isn't good for anyone. Even if the person who abuses you is sometimes nice to you and apologizes for any distress he /she causes you, you still need to end that relationship. It is very common for abusers to apologize and then be very nice and loving towards you after being very abusive. This is a common cycle. If you think your abuser will stop his/her verbal and emotional abuse because he/she is sometimes nice to you or apologizes after being abusive, you are wrong.

Once someone has begun to verbally and emotionally abuse you, especially someone in a relationship with you, it is not likely to stop. In fact, the abuse might become worse.

If you are involved with someone who verbally and emotionally abuses you, you need to end the relationship and get help from a therapist, doctor or social worker so that you can heal your emotional feelings of depression, anxiety and worthlessness.

Dealing with Bullies

We know about bullies at school. Whenever someone bullies us by threatening us verbally and causing us emotional or physical pain on purpose, we know we need to tell a trusted adult as well as our parents. We need to give an adult the names of bullies and details about any bullying incident that might happen at school.

What if you are being bullied at work by adults? How do you respond to bullying by people in other places? Unfortunately, bullies can be anywhere. Bullies can be at school, at work, in the neighborhood, and even in your family.

Bullies might try to take advantage of you, make fun of you in a mean way, trick you for their own enjoyment, threaten you if you don't do what they want, harass you and even physically harm you.

Most people can recognize when they are being bullied. Bullying can happen in a variety of different ways, and bullies can think of many ways to bully, intimidate and threaten you. You might not realize at first that you are being bullied, until you are to the point of being very upset, or scared. It might be ok to ignore bullying at first, especially if ignoring it may make the bully stop his or her intimidation. Learn to recognize it when it happens, so you are prepared to deal with it. The following actions are ways someone could bully you. Some of these actions can be ignored, but some will require you to act on them to stop the bullying.

1. <u>Insults</u> – Someone might repeatedly insult you by saying mean things to you, such as calling you worthless, ugly and stupid and other words like that. A bully can also insult you by making fun of you and embarrassing you. You can usually ignore insults and laugh them off, but if they get to be too much and are especially hurtful, tell the person to stop. Most importantly, don't show him or her that you are upset by any insults, because that will just encourage the bully to insult you more. Bullies want to feel powerful, and seeing you get upset makes them feel powerful. Remember, insults are only words. Try to stay calm and ignore them, if you can. Don't let insults hurt you.

2. Threats – Someone might say that they will hurt you or do something that will upset you. Most threats start with a demand, such as "give me your money." Many times a bully wants something from you, like money, food, a bike, shoes, or something else belonging to you. Sometimes the bully will want you to do something. The bully will then add a threat if you don't give them what they want. The threat might be physical harm to you or damage to your belongings. A threat could also be telling your secrets to others, destroying your reputation, embarrassing you, or hurting someone else who is your friend, pet or family member. The bully will often make a threat to you if you tell anyone else about the bullying. Ignore that threat, no matter how bad it may be, and always tell a parent, trusted adult and friends about any bullying incidents.

Most threats don't actually happen. The bully is hoping the threat will make you do what he/she wants. Don't do what the bully wants you to do, because he/she will continue to demand more from you. Instead, refuse to do what the bully wants and tell the bully to leave you alone. Be prepared in case the bully's threats happen. If the bully attempts to act on his or her threats, tell the bully that if he/she hurts you, damages your property or hurts someone else, you will report him/her to the adults in charge and possibly the police for assault. If the bully threatens to tattle on you or embarrass you, you can laugh it off and tell the bully you will report him/her for threatening you. It's essential that you remain calm when confronting a bully. Remember, don't let the bully see that you are upset by the threats.

3. Intimidation – This is usually anything the bully says or does that causes you to be afraid. Many times intimidation is used with threats. A bully might get in your personal space and give you a mean and nasty look. Sometimes all it takes is a mean, threatening look from a bully to make you feel intimidated. A bully might also have something which could be used as a weapon to scare you or threaten you even more. Sometimes a bully will yell at you and scream hateful, critical words at you. Usually a bully will wait until the two of you are alone before threatening and intimidating you, but if the bully is your boss, he/she will most likely scream at you in front of others.

If your boss is bullying you, it can cause a very tricky situation. A boss is in charge of the work of many people, and a boss can get mad, be demanding and seem mean at times rather than truly being a bully. If a boss is a bully, it is best to ignore his/her tactics of intimidation and try to remain calm. There are measures you can take against your boss, such as talking to a Human Resource representative, a Union Steward (if you are in a union) or another boss. However, doing this can sometimes make matters worse. If you can ignore the behavior of your boss and focus on your work, sometimes that is the best course of action. If your boss is very difficult to work for, you may also want to simply find a different job or ask to be transferred to a different department or shift where you will not have that person as your boss.

If a bully is a co-worker, student or someone else, avoid being alone with that person and document any and all acts of intimidation toward you in case you need to show it to someone in authority. Do not show fear when a bully intimidates you. Calmly tell him/her to stop harassing you, and if he/she doesn't stop, report him/her to someone in authority. If you have co-workers who are friends or who you get along with, focus on maintaining your relationships with those people and ignore and avoid the bullies.

4. <u>Physical acts of violence</u> – This includes any act of physical abuse toward you by a bully. Often these acts of physical abuse may start small: a poke, a pinch, touching you inappropriately, tripping you or spilling things on you. Sometimes these actions can appear to be accidental, but if you notice a pattern of these behaviors, then that should tell you they aren't accidents, but intentional acts of bullying. If you ignore small acts of physical abuse, the bully might do more harmful acts toward you. Don't ignore physical acts of abuse and violence towards you, even small ones. Tell the bully very clearly and seriously to stop bothering you. Make it also clear that you will file a report against him/her and call the police, if necessary, if this abuse doesn't stop immediately. Most states in the U.S. have laws against anyone who bullies someone with a disability, including ASD.

Anyone who bullies someone is insecure and likes to insult others and make them upset in order to feel powerful and better about themselves. Sometimes a bully will do this to gain friends or to look stronger or smarter than you. Sometimes a bully will bother and harass you because he/she thinks you are easy to push around. Many times a bully will purposefully do things to you that will get you upset and cause you to react in a big way. That's why it's essential that you try to remain calm anytime someone bullies you. Think about what you need to do, and try not to get upset. Bullies like to see the people they are bullying get upset, and if they see that they can make you upset, they will bully you more. Bullies do not like to be laughed at or ignored – they want to feel powerful, and someone laughing at them and ignoring them when they try bullying you doesn't make them feel powerful, so simply ignoring a bully will often cause them to give up.

No matter why someone bullies you, you need to know that a bully is not your friend and is not to be trusted. If you can't avoid or ignore a bully, you need to take action against the bully. Act calmly, and try not to show you are upset, when a bully harasses you. Tell the bully to immediately stop whatever he/she is doing to you that constitutes bullying.

Sometimes ignoring a bully doesn't work. If you ignore a bully, he/she may try even harder to get a reaction from you. The bullying may continue and get worse. If the bully doesn't stop and continues to bother you, privately ask friends or co-workers what they think about the situation and how they would handle it. Ask friends and co-workers for advice and support when dealing with someone who is bullying you. You will probably find that most people don't like or trust anyone who is a bully.

Once you know how others feel about the bully, and once you know your co-workers or friends will support you, you should stand up to the bully again, and tell him/her to stop bothering you. Tell the bully that if he/she doesn't stop harassing you, you will take steps to stop him/her. This may be enough to stop the bully.

If the bully continues to bother and bully you, file a complaint with the school principal or employer. Be sure to document, or write down, specific times when you were bullied and exactly what happened. If others have witnessed you being bullied, ask if they would be willing to testify or tell authorities what they saw when you were bullied. If you have enough evidence which clearly shows someone has bullied and taken advantage of you, and the school or workplace have done nothing about it, you should contact the police. Depending upon the amount and severity of the bullying, the police may be able to give the bully a restraining order, which means the bully can't be near you or attempt to bother you in other ways.

If You Are Bullied:

- <u>Stay calm!</u> The bully wants you to get upset. Don't let that happen.
- <u>Be alert and recognize the signs of someone bullying you.</u> Once you know someone is bullying you, you can think about what you need to do.
- <u>Avoid being alone with a bully.</u> Once you know someone is bullying you, stay away from him/her. Be with groups of people and friends as much as possible.
- <u>Talk to parents, trusted adults, and people in authority about any bullying incident.</u> The bully often depends on secrecy to continue to bully you. Once adults or people in authority know about it, he/she won't be able to continue to bully you. Always tell others if someone is bullying you!

> **<u>Ask friends and co-workers for advice about dealing with a bully.</u>** **The more people you have on your side against the bully, the better. You need others to support you and testify for you against the bully.**

> **<u>Document all bullying incidents.</u>** **Write down who bullied you, and when, where, and how it happened. It's important to try to remember as many details about the bullying as possible. This will become important information when you report a bullying incident.**

> **<u>Always tell the bully to stop the harassment immediately!</u>** **It might be scary to stand up to the bully, but at some point you may need to. Be calm and serious when you tell a bully to stop.**

> **<u>Don't scream or use any physical violence against the bully.</u>** **The bully wants you to get upset, and sometimes a bully wants you to attack him/her. If you attack a bully, the bully can use that to say he/she isn't solely at fault and may even accuse you of bullying him/her!**

> **<u>If someone hurts you, the law is on your side.</u>** **It is often against the law to bully someone with a disability, and if you have been hurt physically, you can file assault charges against the bully with the police.**

132

When you take action and get authorities or police involved, that sends a message to the bully to stop bullying and harassing you immediately. Remember, it is unlawful in most states in the U.S. to bully someone with ASD or another disability.

Sometimes people who have been bullied become bullies themselves. Don't let that happen to you! You know that bullies are mean and nasty people. Don't allow yourself to become a bully! Remember, people won't like you and won't be your friend if you are a bully.

Bullying can happen anywhere and at any time. Always let the bully know that you don't like it and you want it to stop immediately. Never use physical violence to deal with a bully! Violence will only make the situation worse and might get <u>you</u> in trouble or even arrested. Just remember, if the bullying doesn't stop, you need to file an official complaint with people in charge, and if the bullying becomes aggressive and dangerous, you should involve the police.

If Someone Hurts You

Unless you physically provoke a person or intentionally harm someone, it is usually never okay for anyone to intentionally hurt you. Self-defense from an attack or defending someone else from a harmful attack is typically the only reason anyone might be allowed to seriously hurt someone else. The rule is this: if you don't intentionally hurt others, people shouldn't hurt you.

In certain sports, such as martial arts, boxing, wrestling, and contact sports such as football, it is okay for competitors to hurt each other, depending on the rules of the sport or game. Every sport has different rules about how players can hurt other players. Sometimes friends might decide to play fight, for fun. When friends fight for fun, they don't really want to hurt each other – they are usually pretending to be famous wrestlers or super heroes, or they may be practicing a martial art like karate. When one of them doesn't want to fight anymore or someone gets hurt, the fight is over. Friends don't actually want to hurt each other.

Sometimes friends might get very angry at each other and may start yelling and shoving each other or even hitting each other. This is more common among adolescents and young children who are still learning to manage their emotions; the older you get, the less acceptable this behavior is. Adults should never get angry and shove or hit people. By the time you are an adult, people will expect you to have learned how to express anger in appropriate ways that do not include hurting others.

If you get angry and hurt a friend, that friend may be very angry with you and not want to be friends with you anymore. You will have to apologize, hope your friend forgives you and try to make sure you never do it again. If you hurt a friend one time or maybe even a couple times, that friend might forgive you and continue to be your friend. If you hurt your friend several times, he/she may decide not to be your friend anymore. Friends don't hurt each other, and they don't want to spend time with people who will hurt them. Likewise, if you have a friend who hurts you, you might forgive him/her, but if he/she hurts you several times, you should probably stop being his/her friend.

No one should hurt you as a punishment, or because you made a mistake or did something wrong. No one should hurt you because they are mad or upset and take their anger out on you. Many people can become physically violent and fight and hurt others, but that doesn't mean it's okay; in fact, it's wrong!

Fighting, especially with weapons, and with the intent to harm someone, is usually illegal. Intentionally destroying or damaging someone else's property is also illegal. If someone hurts you intentionally or threatens to hurt or kill you, you should contact the police and press charges against the attacker.

Domestic abuse happens when your spouse (husband/wife) or a boyfriend/girlfriend intentionally harms you because they are mad at you, or wants to control you. Sometimes a spouse, partner, boyfriend/girlfriend will be verbally abusive to you or threaten to harm you if you don't do exactly what they want. Sometimes a person you live with will become jealous because they think you are spending too much time with others, or he/she thinks you are cheating on them.

No matter why someone is mad at you, even if he/she is your spouse or boyfriend/girlfriend, it is never okay for that person to physically harm you, verbally threaten you or become abusive to you in other ways.

If you are in a relationship with someone who is abusive to you, even if you like that person a lot, you need to end the relationship. Any physical violence and verbal threats of harm in a relationship should tell you that the relationship is bad and dangerous.

If your spouse or partner hurts you or threatens to hurt you, it's important that you contact the police and get help from parents or other trusted adults.

A spouse or partner may hurt you but apologize afterwards and say they will never do it again. You can't believe those apologies, especially if this has happened more than once. It's common in cases of domestic abuse for the abuser to hurt their partner, apologize, hurt them again and apologize, on and on in a cycle that does not end. If your spouse or partner physically and intentionally hurts you once, he/she is likely to do it again. In order to protect yourself from harm, you need to get away from the person hurting you and contact the police as well as trusted adults who can help you.

Likewise, it is not okay for you to hurt anyone. Even if you are very angry or upset, you should not hurt your loved ones, family, friends, teachers, children, neighbors, co-workers, peers, animals or even strangers. The rules apply to everyone. Do <u>not</u> hurt anyone unless you need to defend yourself from someone who intends to hurt you.

Rules to Follow:

1. Don't hurt anyone, even if you are very angry or upset. Being upset with someone is no excuse to hurt them.
2. Don't use any weapons against anyone. Guns, knives, or anything used to hurt someone are considered weapons. Using weapons against a person could get you arrested. Police may need to use weapons against you, if you are using weapons or threatening others with weapons!
3. Don't damage or destroy another person's property, even if you are angry with that person. Destroying someone's property is illegal and can get you arrested.
4. If someone intentionally hurts you, especially if they cause you serious physical harm, tell parents, trusted adults and, if necessary, the police.
5. If someone hurts you out of anger or because you did something wrong, but then apologizes for it afterwards, the apology doesn't count. Intentionally hurting you is assault, and you need to report it to a trusted adult and the police.
6. Realize that if someone hurts you on purpose out of anger, he/she will very likely do it again, no matter how sorry he/she may say they are for those actions.
7. If someone attacks you and physically hurts you, do what you can to defend and protect yourself. As soon as possible, try to get away from anyone who is attacking you. Once you are safely away from an attacker, contact the police.

We hear about people getting hurt by others on TV, in the news and other places. As long as we follow the rules and know what to do if someone hurts us, we should be okay and eventually be safe.

If You Are Mugged

When a person is mugged, it means he/she is assaulted or attacked by one or more people who usually intend to steal something from him/her. A mugger wants to take your money, wallet, purse, cell phone or something else that is valuable from you and will usually threaten you with violence or hurt you to get it. The mugger might have a weapon, like a gun or knife, and will tell you to give him/her your valuable possessions, or else he will hurt you.

Being mugged is a serious and dangerous situation. No one wants to get mugged!

It is usually better to avoid getting mugged in the first place. A mugger doesn't want witnesses during the mugging, so muggers will usually attack people who are alone and isolated from other people. A mugger will usually pick a spot that's dark or secluded, which will further prevent anyone, and you, from seeing him/her. Many muggings happen at night for this reason. A mugger might be waiting behind a building, a car, bushes or something large enough to hide behind for someone to come by, and then mug that person. A mugger might follow you and wait for a good opportunity to mug you.

A mugger will usually look for someone who is distracted and not paying attention to their surroundings. People who are wearing headphones or are looking intently at their phones are usually good targets for muggers. Thieves like to get the things they want quickly and leave, so they are often very fast. They might grab your phone or purse out of your hands and run away. You shouldn't chase them. You might get lost chasing them and end up in a dangerous area with no friendly people around. The mugger may pull out a weapon and hurt you, and there won't be anyone to help you. If a mugger takes something of yours and runs away with it, don't chase them! It is important to try and remember what the mugger looks like and what direction he/she ran so you can tell the police.

A mugger might approach you and ask you a question. Not all people who approach you and ask you a question will be muggers, but it's always a good idea to be cautious anyway. If you are alone and someone approaches you, keep moving quickly, and don't let the person get too close to you.

Safety Tips:

1. Stay in well-lighted and well-populated areas.
2. Stay away from dangerous areas and places that have potential hiding locations for muggers.
3. Walk with others, and try not to walk alone. If you are alone, stay close to others who are walking in your direction.
4. Pay attention to the people and things around you. Look for possible dangers.
5. Don't wear headphones or look at your phone while walking.
6. Don't wear lots of jewelry or carry expensive items such as a watch, handbags, phones and expensive coats/jackets. If you have any expensive things with you, try to keep them hidden or covered up.
7. Don't walk with money or your wallet in your hands.
8. Walk quickly and confidently with purpose.
9. If you have to walk alone, wear shoes and clothes which make it easy for you run or walk quickly.
10. If you live in a high-crime area where there are many muggings, consider taking a self-defense class.

If you are mugged, how you act will depend on the situation. If you are alone and the mugger has a weapon, such as a gun, it is usually better to cooperate with the mugger and give him/her your valuables. Don't argue with the mugger or make him/her mad, or he/she may decide to hurt you. Once you are out of danger from the mugger, run away fast. Go to a safe place, report the mugging to the police, or tell a trusted adult who can help you report the mugging.

If you are mugged and other people are nearby or you can safely run from the mugger, scream for help and run away fast.

Don't go anywhere with a mugger. If a mugger wants you to get in a car or a building or away from a public area where others might be, scream and fight the mugger as best you can. Try to get away from the mugger as soon as possible, and run toward other people.

Always tell the police as soon as possible if you are mugged. If a mugger takes your phone, ask to borrow the phone of someone nearby or go into a nearby store or gas station and ask to use their phone to call 911. Make sure you know where you are, because the 911 dispatcher will ask you where you are. Try to determine what street you are on and what address or building you are in or near. The police will come to you and will want you to describe what the mugger looked like and what direction he/she ran. They may ask you to get in their police car with them to help them find the mugger as they drive around the neighborhood. They might find the mugger or they might not. The police might ask you to come back to the police station with them to file a report about the mugging.

Being mugged is scary and dangerous. A mugging may give you nightmares, and it may take a long time for you to feel comfortable walking outside. If you are ever mugged, be sure to talk to a trusted adult and a therapist to help you feel better and less terrified about your experience.

Appropriate and Inappropriate Touching

Most people will allow brief touching of the hands, shoulder, back or arm. Those are the four areas on a person's body where it's usually okay to touch someone. For example, we touch hands when we give a high five or shake hands. We might touch someone's shoulder or arm to get their attention or give assurance. Sometimes a person will pat you on the back to comfort you, congratulate you or to tell you that you did a good job.

Touching a person's hands, shoulder, arm or back is usually okay. Sometimes a person won't want you to touch them at ALL. Unless it's an emergency, most people won't touch a stranger, even on the back, shoulder or arms. If you are being introduced to someone, it's usually customary to shake hands with that person. That will probably be the only time you touch a person you just met.

People don't typically like to be touched on their heads, chest, legs or feet. Even if you know the person well, such as a co-worker, neighbor, teacher or friend, those areas are usually off limits for touching. A person would feel uncomfortable, confused and possibly angry if he/she is touched on the head, feet, legs or chest by another person.

It is very offensive and considered sexual harassment, molestation, and even sexual abuse if you intentionally touch someone on the butt, between their legs, or on a woman's chest/breasts. The parts of our bodies covered by our underwear are off limits, no matter what a person is wearing. Even if a person is wearing lots of clothing or a coat, it is never okay to touch a stranger, co-worker, peer, sibling, parent, family member, child, friend, or neighbor on his/her genitals, butt or, in the case of girls and women, on their chests.

Sometimes you might accidentally touch someone in a private area. If that happens, move away quickly and apologize. Most people are very careful to avoid touching private, intimate areas on another person's body.

The only time it is okay to touch someone on the private areas of their body is if you are a boyfriend/girlfriend or spouse, and they allow you to touch them intimately. Regardless, even if a girlfriend/boyfriend allows you to touch them intimately in private, it is not appropriate to touch your partner in a sexual way in public.

Kissing and hugging are also ways in which people touch each other. It's usually okay to kiss family members, your boyfriend/girlfriend or your spouse. Kissing anyone else is usually not okay and would very likely be offensive and possibly make that person angry. The same is true for hugging. Most people hug family members, good friends, boyfriends/girlfriends or spouses. Anyone else may find hugging uncomfortable or offensive.

The type of touching that is considered appropriate also depends on the culture or country. In the U.S., it is not common for people to kiss or hug strangers, but in other places, or in other cultures, it might be very normal. If you are visiting another country where people kiss each other on the cheeks or hug to say hello, it's okay to do it too. However, if it makes you uncomfortable, you don't have to hug or kiss anyone! (Most people in other countries will know that people from the U.S. do not kiss cheeks or hug when saying hello, so they will not be offended if you do not do those things.)

If someone touches you briefly on the arm, shoulder, back or hands, it is considered appropriate and acceptable. If you are uncomfortable being touched, even in those socially acceptable areas on your body, let people know. People typically don't want to upset you, and if they know you don't like being touched, they will try to remember that and honor your boundaries by not touching you. If a person touches you in a way that bothers or upsets you, calmly tell them before they attempt to touch you again.

It is very inappropriate for people (other than a spouse or intimate partner) to touch you on private areas of your body, even if you don't mind. If someone intentionally touches you between your legs or on your butt or chest, that is typically considered sexual harassment and molestation. It's also considered inappropriate for someone to touch your underwear (touching or pulling on underwear, snapping bra straps, etc.). Tell anyone who touches you inappropriately to stop immediately and that, if they do it again, you will report them for sexual harassment/molestation.

There are rules to appropriate and inappropriate touching, but if someone touches you in a way that feels too intimate or uncomfortable, it is always okay to tell them to stop. Everyone in the U.S. has the right not to be touched if they don't want to be touched. If someone touches you in any way, and you don't want them to, then you can tell them not to touch you, and they need to comply.

Touching Exceptions:

- If you are a child or under the guardianship of a caregiver or institution where you may need to be touched by parents, teachers or caregivers for your safety or to make sure you are complying with required tasks.
- If you are being apprehended by police, being arrested or are in jail or prison, you lose certain rights, such as your right not to be touched by guards or police.
- If you have signed a document or agreement that removes certain rights of yours, such as the right to not be touched by others. For example, if you sign yourself into a clinic or institution, join the military or take certain jobs, you may sign an agreement that allows for specific people to touch you in certain situations.
- If you are in a hospital, need medical treatment or are in danger of dying. Doctors, nurses, paramedics, lifeguards and people performing CPR or stopping you from choking or bleeding will touch you in order to save your life.

The only people who should touch your private areas are parents/caregivers, and medical workers when they are taking care of your health or grooming out of necessity.

The only people who should EVER touch you in a sexual way are boyfriends/girlfriends and spouses and ONLY when you want them to. Even if you are in prison in the U.S., you still have rights, and you still have the right not to be touched sexually.

Now that you are a young adult, the rules of touching have changed.

- It's usually still okay to touch someone briefly on his/her back, arm, shoulders and hands, unless he/she removes your hand, moves away from you or tells you not to touch him/her.
- If you touch someone on his/her back, shoulder, arm or hand, be sure you have a good reason to do it: gaining attention, comforting, guiding or congratulating. Don't decide to touch someone for no particular reason!
- When being formally introduced to people, it is usually expected that you shake hands, especially if someone puts his/her hand out for you to shake it.
- Don't touch a stranger unless there is an emergency or you need to gain that person's attention.
- If you don't usually like to be touched by people (on your back, hands, shoulders and arms), tell others in a kind, friendly way. Try not to over-react or get angry.
- Sometimes in crowded situations, people are pressed up against each other, and it is necessary for your arms and back to touch another person. That's okay, as long as you don't touch them with your hands.
- Hugging and kissing are also ways people touch each other. Most people are comfortable hugging and kissing family members, spouses and boyfriends/girlfriends. Sometimes friends hug each other when greeting each other or when saying good-bye. You shouldn't hug or kiss strangers or people you don't know well.
- In emergencies or if someone needs to help you with your health or hygiene, it may be necessary to touch you. It is never okay for that person to intentionally touch you in a sexual manner.
- It is never okay for anyone, other than a boyfriend/girlfriend or spouse, to touch you sexually.
- Intimate touching of your genitals, butt and chest by a boyfriend/girlfriend or spouse should only happen in private. Do not touch anyone's genitals, butt or a woman's chest in public.
- Don't touch your own genitals, butt or breasts in public.
- No one should touch you intimately (your genitals, butt or chest) without your consent, no matter what you are wearing – even if you are wearing heavy clothing.
- If someone touches your private areas (genitals, butt or chest) without your consent, even if you are completely dressed, that is considered sexual harassment and possibly sexual molestation.

Sexual Harassment

Sexual harassment is any kind of unwanted sexual behavior delivered from one person to another person. Sexual harassment can be verbal or non-verbal and can include inappropriate physical behavior.

Both men and women can be sexually harassed or cause others to be sexually harassed. Any time someone does something to you of a sexual nature that is offensive, degrading, intimidating and mean, it is considered sexual harassment.

Inappropriate sexual touching is sexual harassment. For example, if someone intentionally touched the private areas of your body, such as your genitals, butt or breasts, even when you have all your clothes on, it is sexual harassment and might even be molestation! Sometimes a person accidentally brushes up against you and touches your breasts or butt. If you know it's an accident and they apologize, then it is not considered sexual harassment. If it happens more than a few times and you think it might be intentional, then inappropriate sexual touching may be occurring.

Sometimes a person touches you in a way that is sexually suggestive or uncomfortable. If a person strokes and rubs your arm or other areas of your body without being asked or touches you too much or for too long, that is considered inappropriate touching and perhaps sexual harassment. Remember the rules of touching: it is generally okay for one person to touch another briefly on the hands, arms, shoulders and back. All other parts of your body should be off limits.

Sometimes sexual harassment can occur if someone doesn't touch you but intentionally gets too close to you and makes you feel uncomfortable. Staring at your private body areas and intentionally getting too close to you to cause you to be uncomfortable and upset is harassment.

If someone asks for a sexual favor or promises to give you a raise, promises to help you with a task or is especially nice to you if you will give him/her sex, that's not only sexual harassment, but also sexual intimidation. Any time a boss, co-worker, student or anyone asks for a sexual favor in exchange for something you want or need, that is sexual harassment and intimidation. Sometimes constantly pressuring you to go on a date can be considered sexual harassment.

If someone sends you texts, emails and photos which are sexually explicit, that is sexual harassment. A person doesn't have to talk to you face-to-face about sex in order for it to be sexual harassment. If someone sends you texts or emails about the sexual activity he/she wants to do with you or asks to have sex with you, that is considered sexual harassment.

Sexual harassment can be verbal comments or non-verbal sounds. If someone makes remarks about your private areas, calls you by a sexual and degrading name or says anything sexual about you that upsets you and makes you uncomfortable, then it is considered sexual harassment. If someone makes suggestive sounds or gestures towards you, such as kissing sounds at you, or hooting/whistling at you suggestively or sexual thrusting at you, that is also sexual harassment.

Rude and inappropriate comments about your sexual orientation are also considered sexual harassment. Asking questions about your sex life or sexual interests or activities is also sexual harassment. It is not okay to ask someone sexual questions unless that person is someone you are dating or married to. Other than a boyfriend/girlfriend or spouse, only a doctor or nurse can ask you questions about your sexual activities, because those questions are related to your health.

Sexual Harassment Behaviors:

- Any inappropriate sexual touching by someone
- Any unwanted rubbing, stroking or touching by someone anywhere on your body
- If someone repeatedly and intentionally stands too close to you, stares at your genitals or breasts, or rubs up against you in a sexual manner
- Saying mean, degrading or rude comments about your sexual orientation
- Repeated questions about your sexual activities and what you like to do sexually
- Telling sexual jokes, teasing you sexually, or telling you sexual stories that make you feel uncomfortable
- Repeatedly pressuring you to go on a date
- Any unwanted sexual content in texts, emails, or sexually explicit photos sent to you
- Calling you a sexual name, even after being asked to stop: Example: pussy, baby doll, sweet cheeks, babe, honey lips
- Repeated comments about your clothing in a sexual way, and you know it's not just a compliment. Example: "You look so sexy in that tight, red outfit"
- Someone other than a spouse or boyfriend/girlfriend talking to you about sex or comments about your breasts, butt or genitals in a sexual way
- Threatening you in a sexual way or telling you what he/she will do to you sexually
- Making suggestive sounds or gestures towards you, such as sexual thrusts, sexual hand gestures, kissing sounds, wolf whistles, and hooting, even after you tell the person to stop
- Any unwelcome sexual behavior toward you, requests for sexual favors and any other verbal or physical sexual behavior

When it is clear to you that someone is intentionally harassing you with uncomfortable, sexual behaviors, you must not ignore it! Instead you need to take action to stop it. First, you need to tell the person who is sexually harassing you to stop immediately. Tell that person that you do not like these behaviors! Tell the person you will need to talk to the police and other people of authority, such as a supervisor, if he/she does not stop harassing you immediately.

If the person continues to sexually harass you, tell your supervisor or teacher and other trusted adults, including parents. Trusted adults will help you file a report with the police, if necessary.

Sexual harassment is unlawful in most states, and you are within your rights to take action to stop it. Remember that sexual harassment is not just uncomfortable for you, but if it goes on too long, it could lead to worse situations, such as sexual abuse

Rape Is a Terrible Crime!

Rape is violent and scary. Rape is a terrible crime.

If someone forces sex on you and makes you have sexual intercourse or perform other sex acts, it is called rape. Rape happens when you don't want sex, but someone forces you to have sex anyway. It is _never_ okay for someone to rape you!

Do not believe what a rapist tells you. A rapist may try to persuade you to have sex, even if you don't want to. Most rapists want to hurt and scare you. A rapist wants to take advantage of you.

Always scream and yell for help if someone tries to rape you. Run away from a rapist as soon as you can.

Always immediately tell the police and trusted adults if someone rapes you or tries to rape you. Even if you are very sad and scared, you must tell a trusted adult and police right away if you are raped.

Being raped can make you feel sad, scared and upset for a long time. If you have been raped, it's always important to talk to a trusted adult, like a social worker or therapist.

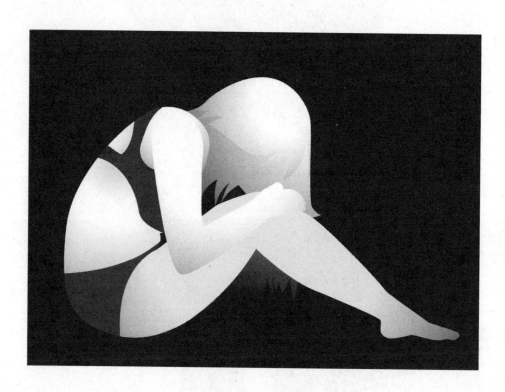

If Raped:

1. Get away from the rapist as soon as you safely can.
2. Once you are safe, immediately call the police.
3. If you don't have a phone, go to the closest place where there are people who can help you. Tell them you need to call the police.
4. Don't change your clothes or clean yourself. Your clothing and body will contain evidence for the police to use.
5. Call your parents or guardian as soon as you can. You will want family members or people you trust with you at the police station or hospital.
6. In most cases, you will be sent to a hospital, depending on how badly you have been hurt.
7. Usually the hospital or police will need to examine you using a rape kit. This will probably be uncomfortable and upsetting. Insist that your parent or a trusted adult stay with you when this happens.
8. The hospital or police will need to remove and keep your clothing as evidence. Make sure your parent brings you more clothes.
9. The police will ask you many questions about the rape. Try to remember as many details as you can: where and when it happened as well as who did it. They will also want to know how it happened step-by-step. Tell the police as much as you can.
10. When you are finished with the police or hospital, go home, shower and put on clean, comfortable clothes.
11. Do not be alone when you go home. Allow parents, family members and friends to comfort you.
12. Don't pretend you are okay, because you aren't. You will need to talk to a therapist, social worker or psychologist possibly many times after your rape experience.

Remember, it is never your fault if you are raped. You are not bad because you were raped. No one ever deserves to be raped. It does not matter where you are, what time of day it is, what you are wearing, or what you are doing. If you are raped, it is never your fault, and it is always a crime.

A person who rapes you is bad. A person who rapes you takes advantage of you and wants to hurt you. A rapist is a criminal who can and should be arrested and put in prison.

Rape is a terrible crime! If you are raped, trusted adults can help you handle it and help you get better. It may take time to emotionally recover from a rape, but with the help of professionals and trusted adults, you will eventually feel happier.

Always immediately call the police and a trusted adult if you are ever raped.

How Rape Happens

Rape happens when someone forces you to engage in a sexual act against your will. Rape happens when you say, "No" and "Stop," but the person doesn't stop and continues to have sex with you anyway. Rape sometimes happens if you are sleeping, or intoxicated, and unable to say you don't want sex. Rape happens if someone forces you to have vaginal or anal intercourse. Rape happens if someone forces you to perform oral sex. Rape can happen to you with one person or two or more people. Rape can happen to you if you are a boy or a girl, a man or a woman. Rape can happen anywhere, at any time.

We usually think a rapist is someone who is a stranger and a bad person who will make you get in his car and take you someplace and rape you. Rape can happen with anyone, and anywhere. Rape can happen in your own home. Unfortunately, rape usually happens from someone you know and possibly even trust. Rape can happen from a boyfriend/girlfriend and even a spouse. Some people think that if you are dating or married, then forced sex cannot be considered rape. This is not true. Any person can rape another person, and it is always a crime.

Anyone can rape you. A neighbor could rape you. A friend could rape you. A family member could rape you. Students, co-workers, your parents' friends, boyfriends and girlfriends can rape you. Most of the people you trust would never force you to have sex and rape you. In certain situations, especially if you are alone with a person, be aware that the person might be capable of forcing you to have sex and rape you.

Sometimes someone could rape you but do not realize they are forcing you to have sex. You must always tell someone "NO" and "STOP" when you don't want sex with them. If you only think you don't want sex with someone and don't tell them, the person having sex with you won't know you want to stop. If you don't say "NO" and "STOP" and try to get away from the person forcing sex, that person may think you are agreeing to have sex with them.

Saying "NO" and "STOP" and fighting the person who is sexually assaulting you or forcefully having sex with you might not stop the rape. By protesting and fighting, you are telling them you do not want to have sex, and they are raping you! It is always important to tell someone having sex with you to stop if you don't want sex, no matter who that person is.

Sometimes a person will try to convince you to have sex. Sometimes a person will trick you into having sex with him/her. A person might promise you money or a gift so you will agree to have sex and not tell anyone. A person might tell you that it's okay to have sex or do what he/she says, because everyone has sex. A person might tell you that you owe them sex or need to have sex with them. You do not ever owe anyone sex, and you do not ever need to have sex with anyone. It doesn't matter what someone tells you or promises you. If you are forced to have sex against your will, it is rape.

Sometimes sexual assault and rape can happen without you being aware of it. If you have had too much alcohol to drink or if you have been given a "date rape" drug, you might not be aware that someone is forcing you to have sex. You may be drunk, drugged or even unconscious and not realize that someone is taking advantage and raping you. That is why it's always advisable not to drink too much, take any kind of drug at a party or drink with someone you don't know well or trust. Don't drink anything from strangers unless you saw it being poured, and always make sure to watch your drink at all times to make sure no one adds anything to it.

Many times a rapist will threaten you. A rapist might tell you he will hurt you or kill you if you tell someone you were raped. If someone has in fact raped you, and is no longer near to hurt you, you must immediately tell several trusted adults, especially your parents, as soon as you are out of danger. It doesn't matter what a rapist says to you; if you are not in immediate physical danger from him, you must tell!

Rape can be very scary, and sometimes even more terrifying, if the rapist has a gun, a knife or another weapon to force you to have sex with him. If someone has a weapon and threatens to hurt or kill you unless you cooperate, you may have to cooperate with the rape. Only cooperate if you are in immediate physical danger and you can't escape.

Always try to escape from a rapist, and if you can, try to fight back! When you escape from a rapist, immediately go to a phone and call the police, and tell any trusted adult you can find who will help you. Immediately tell the police and trusted adults what happened. Tell them you were raped, and give them as many details as you can.

Sometimes rape can happen even if you allow it. Each U.S. state has a law indicating the legal age of sexual consent for that state. For example, if the legal age of consensual sex in a state is 16, then it would be illegal to have sex with anyone younger than age 16. Different states in the U.S. have different ages of consent. If someone over the age of consent has sex with someone under the age of consent, that's considered statutory rape. If someone who is age 18 has sex with someone who is 16, in many states, that's considered statutory rape, even if both partners wanted to have sex with each other. It is important to be aware of the laws of your state so that you do not break any laws. Laws of sexual consent outside of the U.S. vary by country, and if you are traveling to another country, you need to be aware of their laws regarding sex. It is always safest to wait until you are an adult to have sex, and to have sex only with other people who are adults.

If someone forces you to have sex against your will, it is always rape, and rape is a crime. There are no exceptions to this rule. It does not matter if you are married. It does not matter if you wanted sex at first and then changed your mind. It does not matter if you often like to have sex with many people. It does not matter if you were very drunk. You always have the right to refuse sex. If you say no or are unable to say no and someone forces you to have sex, it is rape, and it is a crime.

Even though a rapist may threaten you with harm, you must try to get away from a rapist as soon as you safely can. You must always tell parents, guardians, doctors and the police when you have been raped.

Unit 6: Sex and Sexual Relationships

Introduction to Sex and Sexual Relationships

What Is Sex?

The Rules of Sexual Activity

Having Sex Is a Choice

The Consequences of Unprotected Sex

Can You Get AIDS?

Safe and Responsible Sex

Masturbation Is Private

Deciding to Have Sex with a Partner

When You Are in a Sexual Relationship

Introduction to Sex and Sexual Relationships

Talking about sex and sexual relationships is always complicated and often controversial. In this section I have included some guidelines I think individuals on the autism spectrum need to know about sex and sexual relationships.

I know that many individuals with ASD, especially adults, are sexually active. This may surprise some people, but the truth is that individuals on the spectrum go through the same hormonal changes and have the same sexual drives as anyone else. Furthermore, most of them want intimate relationships with a boyfriend/girlfriend, and some even hope to get married.

Unfortunately, many teens and adults with ASD are naïve about sex and sexual relationships, and it's more likely that they will be taken advantage of as well as abused. It's important that they understand exactly what sex is, with or without a partner, and they understand the rules of sex, including and most importantly, consensual sex.

I frequently emphasize in this section that sex should only be for adults as well as for people who are mature and responsible enough to handle it. The legal age for sex in the U.S. is usually 17-years-old and older, but even at age 17, not all individuals are mature or responsible enough for sex. Being legally old enough for sex also doesn't mean that a person is able to understand and manage the consequences of sex as well as the rules and laws that apply to sex.

Understanding what it means to be protected during sex and taking the steps to ensure that you and your partner are using protection each and every time you have sex is very important. Most responsible adults understand the consequences of having unprotected sex. It's vital that any teenager or young adult who is sexually active, or is soon to be sexually active, understands the importance of protected sex and the consequences of unprotected sex.

It's often the case that well-intended parents try to keep their kids away from information about sex, because they either think their kids with ASD can't handle this information, won't ever need this information or it might give them ideas about what they can do sexually. Parents tend to want to protect their kids from learning too much about topics such as sex, sexual abuse and sexually transmitted diseases. Some parents feel their children wouldn't understand that information or that certain information is too scary for their kids to learn about. Furthermore, many parents are too uncomfortable bringing up these topics with their kids, especially if their kids with ASD ask too many questions about it.

All of this is understandable, which is one of the reasons this book was written. Many kids with disabilities don't get sex education when it is typically taught to students in elementary school or junior high, possibly because they are in a special education classroom at the time, and that information was deemed inappropriate for those students to learn, or they were with mainstream students learning about sex education, but the information was presented in a way that they weren't able to understand. Whatever the reason, most students with disabilities are ill-equipped to understand sex and sexual relationships.

I've been in the position of having to explain information to students who sat in a mainstream classroom but didn't really understand the sex education lessons. Most of the sex information may go over their heads, but the information they do come away with is at times funny, at least to the teachers, but mostly scary for the students. I once had a group of high-functioning boys with ASD in a self-contained classroom, who after listening to a lesson on sexually transmitted diseases was convinced they would get AIDS because a girl in their classroom wore hearing aids. The boys remembered the word AIDS and were not able to distinguish the difference between AIDS and hearing aids. They were afraid they would all die because this girl would give them AIDS. That was the only thing they learned from the 6th grade presentation in a mainstream classroom on sexually transmitted diseases. This is only one of many stories I could share. The point is that we cannot assume that students with disabilities, including ASD, are going to understand the sex education information presented to them, just from listening to a presentation about it. Most of us would agree that they need it presented in a way that they can understand it, with opportunities to ask questions and clarify information. Discussion and clarification are very important. That's why I created a specialized curriculum and taught growth and development, including sex education, for many years to students with disabilities, such as ASD, while they were in elementary school and junior high.

Unfortunately, by the time students with ASD and other disabilities are ready to understand and learn about sex education, which is usually when they are in high school, they don't get the opportunity to learn about it. It's not often taught in high school anymore. And while many neuro-typical high school students have been learning about sex and relationships on their own, their ASD peers haven't necessarily gotten to that point yet. It's not easy for ASD students to catch up to what their teenage peers already know about forming relationships and the complexities of sex.

Nonetheless, parents who are reading this may want to edit or censor some of the information in this section, especially if you feel your teenager is too young or is not yet ready to understand the information presented. This section was written especially for students who are older teenagers or young adults, as well as those who are at risk to become sexually active and may need to know this information. Furthermore, the language and vocabulary in this section is intentionally more difficult and may need to be modified for students who might have difficulty understanding it.

Decide what your children or students need to know from this section, and present it in a way that they can understand and use it.

Tips for Teachers/Instructors:

- Use a modified curriculum and make it a point to teach sex education in junior high or high school to students with ASD and other disabilities.
- If you can't teach ASD students about sex education, at least allow them to learn and discuss specific topics regarding sex, etc., in small support groups.
- Make sure students with ASD and other disabilities understand the rules of sex, including the consequences of sex and the importance of consensual sex.

Tips for Parents:

- Use the information in this book to teach about and discuss sex and sexual relationships with your teenager with ASD.
- Make sure your teen understands the rules and laws regarding any sexual activity, especially as they pertain to him/her.
- Make sure your teen understands that sex is a choice and that sex should always be consensual.
- Have conversations with your teen or young adult about recognizing when people want to take advantage of them sexually.
- Find out who they are dating and hanging out with. Pay attention to any indications from your teen or young adult that they want to be or are becoming sexually active.
- If you know your teen or young adult is masturbating and is not being private about it, remind them to do it in the privacy of their bedroom or bathroom with the door shut and not to discuss it with anyone.
- Make sure your teen or young adult understands the consequences of unprotected sex, and if/when they are sexually active, that they always use protection.

Tips for Teens and Young Adults with ASD:

- Don't even consider becoming sexually active with a partner until you are an adult and mature and responsible enough to handle a sexual relationship.
- Do not have a sexual relationship with someone who is much older or much younger than you.
- Even if you like someone very much, you should wait until you know a person well and can trust that person before having a sexual relationship with him/her.
- Know the rules and laws that pertain to any sexual activity.
- Keep any masturbating activity private and discreet. Don't discuss your masturbation with anyone.
- Know the consequences of sexual activity with a partner, and always be protected with a condom when engaging in any sexual activity.
- Never engage in any sexual activity with a partner unless both of you are of legal age and you both consent to it.

What Is Sex?

There's a lot of disagreement, even among experts, about what sex is. In fact, the word sex can be confusing, because it can have more than one meaning. For example, if someone talks about a person's or animal's sex, they usually mean its gender, either male or female. Having sex typically means that you and another person engage in sex together, usually sexual intercourse. When you hear the term "sex life," that is usually referring to a person's sexual activity with or without partners.

For the purpose of this book, sex can be defined as any physical stimulation or activity involving a person's genitals for the intention of sexual stimulation and sexual orgasm, or release.

When people think about sex, they usually think about sex between a man and a woman. It's possible to have sex with yourself as well as sex with more than one person (group sex). Some people are attracted to others of the same sex or gender. Men who are attracted to other men and choose to have sex with men are called gay or homosexual. Women who are attracted to other women and choose to have sex with women are called lesbian, gay or homosexual. People who are attracted to and like to have sex with people of both the male and female genders are called bisexual.

When a man and a woman have sexual intercourse, it usually means the man puts his penis in the woman's vagina. Typically, the man will thrust his penis into the woman several times and ejaculate his sperm into the woman's vagina. This may cause the woman to become pregnant if she isn't on birth control or if the man isn't wearing a condom during sex. This is how babies are made.

Some people think sexual intercourse is the only definition of sex, but that's not true. If you stimulate yourself to sexual release or orgasm, that's called masturbating. Sex between two or more people can also include anal sex and oral sex. Sometimes genitals are stimulated with a mouth, sometimes with a hand and sometimes with other objects. People may do a variety of unusual things for sexual stimulation, but they all would still be defined as having sex.

A potential sex partner may tell you that oral stimulation to his/her genitals isn't really sex, or that using your or your partner's hand to stimulate his/her genitals isn't sex. That's not true. If you or your partner do anything to your genitals with the intention of sexual stimulation and possible orgasm, then you are engaging in sex.

Deep kissing, mouth-to-mouth, even for a long time, may be stimulating and might even cause you and your partner to become sexually aroused, but it is not considered sex. Kissing may be a prelude or the start of a sexual activity, but it isn't by definition having sex.

If you and your partner touch each other or massage each other without touching your genitals or a woman's breasts, it may feel stimulating and arousing, but it isn't by definition sex.

If you and your partner watch pornography together or read a pornographic book, you may feel genital stimulation and arousal. If neither of you actually touch or stimulate your own or your partner's genitals, then you aren't technically having sex.

If the private parts of your body, such as your genitals, breasts and butt, are involved in direct stimulation, then you can probably say you are participating in a sexual activity or having sex. Most experts would agree to this definition of sex.

Remember, sex is any physical stimulation or activity involving your genitals, by you or someone else for the intention of sexual stimulation and sexual orgasm. During sex, you can sexually stimulate yourself or someone else, and someone can sexually stimulate you. No matter what you do for sexual stimulation, if your or someone's genitals are physically involved, that is considered sex.

The Rules of Sexual Activity

There are many kinds of sexual activity, and the rules for sex apply to all of them. Sexual activity of any kind should only be for adults. You should be an adult, or at least over the age of consent, before you are allowed to have sex with another person. In most states in the U.S., anyone under the age of 17 is considered a child, and sex with a child is against the law. People who are married and adults who are in love typically have sex, but sex is never allowed for children!

Sexual intercourse is a very private and intimate activity between two adults who are usually in love and who agree to have sex with each other. Sex is private. You don't share your sexual experiences with others. Sex is typically not a topic that is publicly announced to a group or discussed with co-workers or acquaintances. Sex is between you and your sexual partner, and it should be private. No one needs to know about the details of your sex life.

Some people believe that sex should only be for married people. This may be a personal or religious belief. Most people think that, once you are married, you should only have sex with your spouse. Adultery happens if you are married but you have sex with someone who is not your spouse. Adultery can often lead to divorce and the end of a marriage. Even if you aren't married, if you cheat on your relationship partner and have sex with someone other than your boyfriend/girlfriend, your relationship will probably end. If you are in a loving, sexual relationship with someone but have sex with someone else, that typically goes against the rules of your relationship.

There are risks to sexual activity with a partner, including pregnancy and sexually transmitted diseases. Whenever you participate in a sexual activity with a partner, you need to take certain steps to be safe and responsible. Women should use a form of approved birth control, and men should always use condoms every time they have sex with a partner. Condoms are very important to prevent the spread of disease, so even if a woman is using birth control to avoid pregnancy, unless you have been with your partner for a while and know they are disease free, men should still use condoms. The exception to this rule is when a couple chooses to get pregnant, in which case you should decide together as a couple if you want to get pregnant before attempting pregnancy.

Sex is something that adults may choose to do. Having sex should always be a choice that an adult may decide to make. No one is allowed to force you to have sex with them. If you don't want sex, no one can tell you that you must have sex. Forcing you to have sex against your will is considered rape, and no matter who the person is, if you are forced to have sex, that is rape, and rape is a crime! A person who commits rape or attempts to sexually assault someone else can be prosecuted and imprisoned. You must always tell the police as well as a trusted adult if someone sexually assaults you or forces you to have sex with him/her.

Even if you agree to have sex with someone but are underage, it is against the law! The age of consent for sexual activity varies by state and country, but in the U.S. the age of consent is usually 16, 17 or 18. Children under the age of consent are never allowed to participate in sex or watch sex. That is illegal, and adults will be arrested if they have sex with a child that is younger than the age of consent. Child pornography is against the law. Anyone who watches child pornography or who buys, sells, produces or downloads child pornography will be arrested and put in prison!

Masturbation is self-stimulation, or sex with yourself. If you rub your own genitals for sexual release, whether you are clothed or not, that is considered masturbation. Many people masturbate, but masturbation is a very private behavior. You should only masturbate in the privacy of your own home, in your bedroom or bathroom with the door closed. Masturbation is also a very private topic and shouldn't be discussed with anyone. Not only is masturbation very private, but it is usually illegal to masturbate in public. You can be arrested or fined for masturbating in public places, because it is considered indecent exposure and lewd behavior. If you masturbate in the presence of children or anyone 16-years-old or younger, you could also be charged with a sexual offense!

It is best not to take photos or video-tape your consensual, sexual activity. If photos or video-tape of your sexual activity leave the privacy of your home or are seen by others, or even worse, put on the Internet, your sex life will no longer be private. If photos of your sexual activity are shared with others or possibly seen on the Internet by everyone you know, that will be extremely embarrassing! It could also ruin your reputation, your relationships with others and your relationship with your intimate partner as well as negatively affect your work or school life.

If you take photos or record someone else having sex without their knowledge or approval, you can be charged and arrested for invasion of privacy. Moreover, you can be sued if you take photos or record someone's sexual activity and post it online or attempt to sell it.

Paying people to have sex with you or selling your sexual services (accepting money or gifts and favors by agreeing to have sex with someone) is called prostitution. Prostitution is illegal in most of the United States. It is only legal in licensed brothels in Nevada. You can be arrested, fined and possibly jailed for buying or selling sexual services.

When it comes to safe and legal sexual activities, there are rules and laws as well as consequences that must be taken into consideration. Remember to abide by these rules and laws regarding any sexual activity.

- Sex should only be for adults! You need to be over the age of consent in order to engage in any form of sex.
- If you are married or in a loving relationship and have sex with someone else, you risk ending your marriage or relationship.
- Keep your sexual activity private. Don't discuss your sexual activity with others, and don't take photos or record any sexual activity.
- Unprotected sex might result in pregnancy and/or contracting sexually transmitted diseases.
- Always use safety precautions when you have sex. Women should use an approved form of birth control to prevent pregnancy, and men should use condoms to prevent pregnancy and infections. The exception to this is when a couple decides together to get pregnant.
- Sex is always a choice. No one is allowed to force sex on anyone. If someone is forced or persuaded to have sex against his/her will, that is considered rape, and rape of any kind is a crime.

- It is illegal to have sex with children and anyone under the age of consent. Children are not allowed to view sex or participate in any form of sex. Having sex with children is considered rape, even if the underage person consents to it.
- Child pornography is illegal. You will be arrested and imprisoned if you produce, buy, sell or download child pornography.
- Masturbation needs to be private. If you masturbate in public places you may be fined or arrested.
- Prostitution is illegal in most of the United States. If you buy or sell sexual services, you can be arrested and jailed.
- It is illegal to photograph or record anyone's sexual activity or nudity without his/her permission. Furthermore, you can be sued by someone if you take photos or record video of him/her undressing or engaging in sex without his/her permission.

Sexual activity with a partner should only be for adults, even if you are of legal age for sex. In order to have sex with someone, it is necessary that you understand the rules and laws of sex and that you have the maturity and responsibility to protect yourself and your partner whenever you have sex.

Having Sex Is a Choice

Having sex is an activity that only adults should participate in. Even if you are over the age of consent and by law can have sex, you should wait until you are an adult and can deal with the effects and consequences of sex. You should have maturity, responsibility and a loving commitment from a partner before you make the decision to start having sex.

Most importantly, having sex of any kind is always a choice. All adults can choose to have sex or not to have sex. This is your right as a consenting adult, and no one has the right to make you have sex once you have decided to stop.

Whatever form of sex you engage in with a partner, it's essential that there is always consent by all participants before sex and that both partners are safe and using appropriate protection. The only appropriate form of sex is between consenting adult people. No matter how you are having sex or who you are having sex with, it is important to remember that everyone participating must want and decide to do it. You can always say "no" to sex, and it is never too late to tell your partner that you don't want to continue once you started having sex.

If you start having sex with a partner and your partner says he/she does not want to have sex anymore, you must stop having sex. Likewise, if you are having sex with someone and you decide you no longer want to have sex, say so, and the other person needs to listen to you and stop. It does not matter if the other person is someone you are dating, someone you are married to or someone you "owe a favor to," no one is allowed to make you have sex against your will. If they do, it is called rape. Remember, rape is illegal and can result in the rapist being arrested and going to prison.

Sometimes you may be with someone who will want to have sex with you very much, and they may tell you that you need to have sex with them, that you owe them sex or that if you really liked them or loved them, you would have sex with them. No matter what a person says to you to convince or force you to have sex with them, it is never okay. It is not okay to try to persuade someone to have sex with you if he/she doesn't want to. If someone tries to persuade you to have sex when you don't want to, that person is trying to take advantage of you, and that person isn't thinking about what you want or what is good for you. What that person is doing is wrong.

Sex should ALWAYS and ONLY happen between people who are over the age of consent and who both want to have sex. It should also only include the sexual acts that a person wants to participate in. If someone wants to only have oral sex, it is not okay to try to make them have vaginal or anal sex. Both participants need to agree on what kind of sex they want to have with each other.

Remember, sex by law is a choice consenting adults can make. No one should be forced to have sex. No one is allowed to force or persuade you to have sex against your will, and you should never force or persuade someone to have sex with you if that person doesn't want to.

The Consequences of Unprotected Sex

Unprotected sex with someone can result in serious health conditions as well as life-changing consequences.

Pregnancy is a life-changing consequence if a man and a woman have unprotected sex together. If you are a married, engaged or committed couple in a long-term relationship, you may decide together to get pregnant. No matter what your relationship is with your sexual partner, you need to understand that becoming pregnant and having a child together is a huge responsibility for both the baby's father and mother.

Becoming pregnant has its own health risks for the baby and the pregnant woman. If you are a woman and you become pregnant, you need to see a doctor, usually an obstetrician. That's typically the first thing a woman does when she discovers she is pregnant. A doctor will monitor the pregnancy to keep the baby and the mother healthy and check on the progress of both.

Typically, the first sign of pregnancy for a woman is a missed menstrual period. If you have missed your period and you suspect you are pregnant, you can buy a pregnancy test at a drug store or make an appointment with your doctor to be sure. Once you know you are pregnant, you and the baby's father have many important decisions to make regarding the future of your relationship and this unborn baby.

If you are a man, and a woman gets pregnant as a result of unprotected sex with you, then you have responsibilities not only to the baby, but to the pregnant mother as well. If that baby is born, you will become a father, and you will be financially responsible for that child to some extent. Having and raising children is expensive and a huge responsibility! Parents are responsible for their children's lives and welfare and will need to pay for almost all of their child's needs until their child becomes an adult. The cost of having and caring for a child is not only expensive, but also long-term, possibly for the rest of your life.

Another consequence of unprotected sex is the possibility of contracting a sexually transmitted disease or infection. Most sexually transmitted diseases (STDs), and sexually transmitted infections (STIs) are contracted by having unprotected vaginal, anal or oral sex with another person.

If you don't want to get pregnant or contract an STD, it's important that you and any sexual partner take safe and responsible precautions each and every time you have any form of sex. This means that sexually active women should have an approved form of birth control, prescribed by a doctor. And men should always use a condom whenever they have sex with anyone. If a couple is in a serious relationship and they know that they are going to be having sex with only each other and that neither of them have any STDs or STIs, then they may decide to no longer use condoms as long as the woman is still using birth control. The types of birth control that are going to be used should be discussed and agreed upon by sexual partners before they have sex.

Only a doctor can diagnose and treat a sexually transmitted disease (STD) or sexually transmitted infection (STI). Not all STDs/STIs are curable, but they are all treatable, and as soon as you know you have an STD/STI, you need to see a doctor. Most STDs/STIs affect both men and women and can be passed from either to men or to women during sex. If left untreated, an STD/STI can cause serious health problems and, in some cases, can potentially cause death. If you are sexually active, and especially if you have more than one sex partner, you will need to get regular check-ups by your doctor to be sure you don't have an STD or STI.

Common Sexually Transmitted Diseases:

Chlamydia is a common STD/STI that men and women can get. It is treatable and curable, but if left untreated, it can cause damage to a woman's reproductive organs and cause a woman to get Pelvic Inflammatory Disease. The symptoms of Chlamydia are unusual discharge from the penis or vagina, a fever and possibly abdominal pain.

Genital Herpes is a contagious infection (STI) caused by a virus. Genital herpes is treatable but not curable. A symptom of genital herpes is usually painful blisters on your genitals or anus, which come and go when you have outbreaks of the virus. The virus outbreaks, especially the first outbreaks, can sometimes occur with a fever.

HIV/AIDS is caused by a virus and can be passed to men and women during sex as well as passed through blood and other body fluids. The HIV virus destroys a person's immune system, making it almost impossible for a body to fight even simple infections. If left untreated, HIV can become AIDS and eventually lead to death. This STD is not curable, but it is treatable.

Human Papillomavirus (HPV) is a very common and contagious STD/STI. Both men and women can get it, and there are 40 different types of HPV. Most doctors will recommend that school-age children, and especially teenagers, get vaccinated to protect against getting HPV. It usually has no symptoms, but once you get this virus, there is no cure. If left untreated, it can cause cervical cancer, vaginal cancer, anal cancer and vulvar cancer.

Trichomoniasis is an infection caused by a parasite. It can affect sexually active women and occasionally men. Symptoms may include genital itching, painful urination, and vaginal discharge. Men can be infected but not have any symptoms. An antibiotic is the typical treatment for this STI, but re-infection can occur if both sex partners aren't treated. Trichomoniasis is very dangerous for pregnant women and unborn babies.

Viral Hepatitis is a serious liver disease that can be caused by several different viruses (Hepatitis B, C and D) which can be passed from one person to another, including during sex. Symptoms might include fatigue, fever, aches and pains and loss of appetite. A vaccination can prevent most forms of Hepatitis, but if left untreated, viral Hepatitis could cause liver damage, liver disease and liver cancer.

Syphilis is caused by bacteria and can be passed during any form of sex with either men or women. The first symptoms of syphilis are painless genital sores. It can be cured with specific medication, but if left untreated, syphilis can affect other organs in your body, for both men and women, and potentially cause death. Women who have syphilis might have a miscarriage or give syphilis to their unborn babies. If you have syphilis, you can more easily contract HIV.

<u>Gonorrhea</u> is caused by bacteria and affects both men and women. The symptoms of gonorrhea are a discharge from the penis or vagina and painful urination. Gonorrhea can also infect a person's mouth, throat, eyes and rectum. Gonorrhea is a curable STD, but if left untreated, it can cause serious health problems, including Pelvic Inflammatory Disease and infertility in women. It is also very dangerous to pregnant women.

Any STD/STI can cause serious health problems if ignored and left untreated. If you have unprotected sex, and especially if your partner thinks he/she has an STD/STI, you should get yourself checked by a doctor.

Deciding to have sex with someone is not something you should consider without serious thought. There are serious consequences to having unprotected sex with someone. Having sex with a partner should always be done with maturity, safety and responsibility.

Can You Get AIDS?

AIDS is a dangerous disease that people can possibly get. The letters AIDS stand for Acquired Immunodeficiency Syndrome. AIDS is caused by a virus called HIV, which is short for Human Immunodeficiency Virus.

The Human Immunodeficiency Virus (HIV) can be passed from one person to another only through the exchange of certain body fluids (liquids in our body). Blood, semen, breast milk, vaginal fluids and rectal fluids from a person with HIV are the only fluids that can give you HIV, and only if they enter your body.

You can't get HIV/AIDS by shaking someone's hands or hugging someone with AIDS. You can't get HIV/AIDS by sharing toilets, towels, drinking cups, plates or eating utensils with anyone. You can't get HIV/AIDS from animal or insect bites.

Most of the time, the HIV virus is passed during sex. This is why AIDS is called a sexually transmitted disease. If anyone has unprotected sex with someone who has HIV, he/she might get the HIV virus too. Protected sex with someone means a man is wearing a condom on his penis during sex. A condom will prevent the virus from getting into the body of the sexual partner. However, most people will not choose to have sex with someone who has the HIV virus.

When people first began getting the AIDS disease in the 1980s, people would often die from it, because doctors didn't know how to help them. They also didn't know how the disease was given from one person to another at first. Some people contracted AIDS from dirty syringes used for giving or taking blood or when they gave themselves injections of illegal drugs. This is why, when you get a shot from the doctor, the nurse always opens up a brand-new, clean syringe.

We now know how people get HIV/AIDS, and because of HIV/AIDS, doctors, dentists and other health care providers are careful to wear gloves when they are touching patients. Doctors now check donated blood and throw away used syringes to prevent anyone from getting the HIV virus.

Today, many people have the HIV virus, but because doctors know how to treat it, most people don't get AIDS and die. People still must be very careful to have protected sex by using condoms, because we can still get HIV from sexual contact.

If people think they might have HIV, they should go to their doctor and get tested. If a doctor knows you have the HIV virus, he/she will tell you what you need to do to prevent getting AIDS and how to not give the HIV virus to someone else.

AIDS is still a scary and dangerous disease, but most doctors in the world know how to help people with HIV virus and prevent AIDS. Unless you are having unprotected sex, you will probably not get HIV/AIDS.

Safe and Responsible Sex

Before having sex of any kind with a partner, you need to be prepared to make your sexual experience safe and responsible. Being safe and responsible means that, during sex, both partners are protected against the consequences of sex, and neither partner is in danger of being physically hurt.

A man should always use a condom during sex to protect him and his partner against any sexually transmitted diseases and possible pregnancy. Condoms can be purchased in almost any drug store, by both men and women, as well as online. You don't need to show identification to buy condoms, but if you are clearly too young for sex, the people at the store may question you about buying them. Some stores might have a policy of not selling condoms to people who are underage for sex. Condoms can also be obtained for free from many health clinics and nurses offices.

Each condom comes in a small foil or plastic wrapped container. When a man is ready for sex, he opens the wrapped container, puts his erect penis in the open end of the condom and rolls the condom down the full length of his penis. Your penis must be erect and ready for sex before you can put on a condom. The entire penis must be covered in the thin rubber of the condom, and there will be a small extra space at the very end of the condom to contain your sperm. The condom will feel tight, but it should feel comfortable. You or your sex partner can put on your condom. After you ejaculate into the condom during sex, carefully roll it off your penis and throw it away. If you choose to have sex again, you must put on a new condom.

It is the responsibility of both men and women to have condoms before sex. Women shouldn't always assume men will have and use condoms during sex. Responsible women will have condoms with her for her male partner during any sexual activity.

Women should also have an approved form of birth control to protect against any unwanted pregnancy during sex. There are different types of birth control for women, all of which can be prescribed by a doctor. These can include injections, implants, pills or items to be inserted into a vagina prior to sex. Get a medical exam and discuss with a doctor what type of birth control is best for you. This involves making a doctor's appointment. During the appointment, a doctor will probably conduct a brief vaginal exam or ask you questions regarding your sexual activity. The doctor will also explain anything you need to know

about your birth control and how to use it. If there is ever a problem with your prescribed birth control, you need to contact your doctor.

Some people like to engage in potentially dangerous activities during sex for more intense sexual stimulation or orgasm. Think carefully about engaging in any sexual activity which might be dangerous to either you or your partner. It would be advisable not to do anything painful, dangerous or life-threatening to yourself or your partner before, during or after sex.

If you suspect that something you or your partner want to do sexually is dangerous, don't take the chance and try it. Always discuss it with your partner, but if a sexual activity is dangerous or potentially harmful, it would be best to just avoid it. No sexual activity is worth any harm to you or your partner.

Having safe and responsible sex means that you will be responsible not only for yourself, but for your partner as well. It means that both of you are protected against any sexually transmitted diseases, as well as possible pregnancy. It also means you are keeping yourself and your partner safe from any potentially harmful sexual activities.

Masturbation Is Private

Masturbation is typically defined as stimulating your own genitals for sexual pleasure. Some people regard masturbation as an immoral and improper form of sexual activity, but masturbation is actually a natural form of sexual stimulation and nothing to feel guilty about. Most people have engaged in masturbation at some point in their lives, either accidentally or intentionally, and that is normal. Adolescent boys and young men tend to masturbate more than most people, but masturbation behavior is not limited to them. Adolescent girls and women will also intentionally masturbate.

The understood rules for masturbation are simple. Masturbation is considered a very private sexual activity and something you do alone in private, in your bedroom or bathroom. Furthermore, it's so private that you usually don't discuss masturbation with anyone. Most people would be embarrassed if others knew about their masturbation behavior.

How often you masturbate and how you masturbate are private issues and something you shouldn't share with anyone. However, if you are masturbating a lot and it becomes the main activity you need to do or look forward to doing every day, then your masturbating may be a problem.

If you are masturbating excessively, you need to find out why. Masturbating too much could be caused by anxiety or stress, and you may be masturbating to relieve your anxiety. You may also be masturbating a lot due to a sexual obsession. Masturbation can be addictive, and it's possible to hurt yourself if you masturbate too much or too vigorously. If you are masturbating several times a day or masturbating too vigorously to the point that you are hurting yourself, you need to talk to a doctor and possibly a psychologist.

The law regarding masturbation is that it is not allowed in public places, and that's another reason to keep masturbation private and restricted to your own home in the privacy of your bedroom or bathroom. Masturbating in public places is considered indecent exposure and lewd public behavior. You can possibly be arrested and fined for masturbating in public.

Masturbation is a perfectly normal form of sexual stimulation. Remember to only masturbate in the privacy of your bedroom and bathroom, and don't discuss your masturbation with anyone. Don't masturbate too often or until you cause yourself injury. If you become obsessed with masturbation and think about it constantly or masturbate several times a day, you need to contact your doctor.

Deciding to Have Sex with a Partner

Sex is always a choice. It's a choice consenting adults can make. If you are not an adult, you should not make the choice to have sex. If your partner is not an adult, you should not consider having sex with that person, even if that person says yes.

Sex involves a lot of responsibility and maturity, which is why it should only be for adults. It's a choice that consenting adults can agree to make. Sex is never for children. Children should never participate in any physical sex, talking about sex or watching sex. Sex is only for adults who decide to engage in sex.

Sex is a very intimate act. Deciding to have sex should be a serious, thoughtful decision. Having sex may feel good to you, but it can also result in serious consequences.

Having sex can result in pregnancy. A woman can get pregnant when she has sexual intercourse with a man. If you are a woman, you should be on an approved form of birth control and have condoms for your male partner to use. If you are a man, you should use condoms each and every time you have sex.

Having sex can cause you to get a sexually transmitted disease, such as chlamydia, genital herpes, gonorrhea, syphilis, or AIDS, if your sexual partner has a sexually transmitted disease, which he/she can pass on to you. Sexually transmitted diseases can be very dangerous and long lasting.

Furthermore, having sex can result in physical injury if you or your partner do something sexually which would cause you physical harm. Avoid doing anything painful or dangerous during sex.

You need to be safe and responsible for your body at all times when you decide to have sex. Your sexual partner also needs to be safe and responsible before, during and after you have sex.

Having sex with someone you love very much can be a wonderful and fulfilling experience. People who love each other enough to get married will usually enjoy a love-filled sexual experience.

Having sex with someone can also cause emotional upset and may result in major changes to a relationship. Sometimes having sex with someone can end a friendship or relationship.

Having sex with someone doesn't mean that person loves you. Sex and love can go together, but they are not the same. A person can have sex with you but not love you. Always know why a person wants to have sex with you and why you want to have sex with that person. Do not allow anyone to take advantage of you by insisting on having sex with you.

Always think about whether you want sex or not. Think about the possible consequences of sex before you decide to have sex with someone.

Questions to Ask Yourself and Partner Before Having Sex:

1. Am I an adult and old enough and responsible enough to have sex?
2. Is my possible sex partner an adult and responsible enough to have sex?
3. Do my sex partner and I both consent (say yes) to having sex?
4. Do I understand what will physically happen when I have sex with a partner?
5. Am I emotionally and mentally prepared to engage in this physical act of intimacy with someone?
6. Am I making the choice by myself to have sex, or is someone trying to convince me?
7. Am I being safe and responsible for me and my partner to have sex?
8. Do I personally have protection, such as a condom and other birth control, against possible pregnancy or sexually transmitted diseases?
9. Have I been intimate in other ways besides sex with my partner, such as hugging, kissing, talking about intimate feelings toward each other and experiencing a close, trusted relationship?
10. Do I know what will possibly happen to my relationship with my partner after we have sex? Have I talked about this with my partner?

You should answer yes to all of these questions before you are ready to engage in sex with your partner.

Other things to consider and ask yourself:

How do I feel about my partner, and does my partner feel the same way about me? After having sex with this person, what could happen next, and what will I do?

Having sex with someone can be a wonderful experience, but it is always a serious decision involving consent (saying yes) every time, as well as safety and responsibility. It's important to think carefully before deciding to have sex with someone.

When You Are in a Sexual Relationship

If you are in a committed sexual relationship with someone, hopefully someone you love, it can be very satisfying and healthy for both you and your partner.

When you have a sexual relationship with someone, it typically means you are not only intimate with each other, but also know a lot about each other. It requires you to have communication with your partner and a good understanding about what your partner wants and expects. You won't be able to sustain a sexual relationship if you can't be intimate with each other and communicate at least adequately.

In most sexual relationships, the boundaries of touch and privacy are almost gone. You have to expect that your partner will want to touch you in a familiar, caring and intimate way, and you should expect that you will touch your sexual partner the same way. Sometimes sexual partners establish rules about intimacy, touching and public displays of affection. This is perfectly fine, assuming you both create and agree to the rules together.

Depending on where you will be having sex with your partner, you need to assume that you will probably be sharing a bathroom and bedroom. The boundaries of privacy in those areas will also have to be established. Perhaps you don't want your partner to share your bathroom, towels, soap or toothbrush. Maybe you don't want your partner to share your bed and use your favorite pillow. This can be a problem if you have a sexual relationship. Be prepared to share your space, and be sure you don't insult or hurt your partner's feelings by enforcing strict rules of privacy and property. Communicate with your partner, and be prepared to discuss what's important to you in a gentle and thoughtful way.

If you have unusual rituals, obsessions or habits, it's best to let your partner know before they happen. Talk about what's important to you and what you both need before you become intimate with each other. Everyone has personal, private rituals and behaviors, which they might be uncomfortable showing anyone else. A lot of misunderstandings can happen when people are with each other in their private spaces while engaging in private behaviors. Always talk about those behaviors before either of you becomes angry, upset, disgusted or insulted.

Some people are more private than others when it comes to sharing space, talking about their needs and even being naked with someone. This is to be expected. You are two different people, and it's very likely you will find you have different ideas about privacy, personal needs and expectations. Try not to argue or be demanding. Work toward a friendly compromise if there is ever a disagreement, and try to be understanding of your partner's needs and feelings. Respect your partner, and be sure your partner respects you.

When it comes to actually having sex together, remember to let your partner know what you like and learn what your partner wants, so that you are both sexually satisfied. If only one partner receives sexual satisfaction while having sex, that is inconsiderate and not good for the relationship. A sexual relationship will not last if one partner is not enjoying it and not achieving sexual satisfaction. Have an open and honest discussion about what you both like to do sexually as well as what you both are uncomfortable doing. It's a good idea to talk occasionally with your partner about your sex life together and even make changes if your sex becomes too routine.

Sexual and loving relationships can be hard work and may need constant attention. Expect that disagreements and occasional jealousies will happen, and be prepared to discuss them openly and honestly.

Sexual Relationship Suggestions:

- Talk with your partner about your and his/her expectations. Recognize that you are both different people and probably have different ideas regarding your sexual relationship.
- Talk about intimate touching and displays of public affection together. Decide what you are comfortable with.
- Expect to share space and items, and talk about that.
- Talk to your partner about any habits, rituals or unusual behaviors you have that he/she needs to know about. Ask your partner to talk to you about habits, rituals and his/her behaviors as well.
- If you need to establish rules, create them together with your partner. No one enjoys being told what to do and how to do it without being a part of the decision-making. If you or your partner are too bossy and make all the rules, your relationship won't last.
- Listen to what your partner says regarding his/her wants and needs, acknowledge those needs and discuss them together. And make sure your partner listens to and discusses your needs.
- Always try to respect your partner and be honest with each other. When you have honesty and respect, you will also have trust, and trust in a sexual relationship is important.
- Be sure you are both sexually satisfied when you have sex together. Don't assume your partner is satisfied just because you are.
- Constant fighting and jealousy is a "red flag," or indication that the relationship isn't healthy. If you can't discuss at least most disagreements rationally, you may need to end the relationship. End the relationship if there is any reoccurring physical abuse.
- If your partner is frequently verbally and emotionally abusive to you, end the relationship.
- Don't share intimate details about your sexual partner or your relationship with others. Keep your intimate relationship private.
- Be sure to always have safe and responsible sex, and be sure you and your partner are protected.

Above all, in any sexual and/or loving relationship, you need to listen carefully to what your partner needs and wants and be open to discussion and compromise. A good sexual relationship is an equal relationship. You both need to be honest with each other and respect each other. In a good relationship, you each need to trust each other; trust that you and your partner will listen to each other, talk to each other, and be kind and caring to each other. This is important if you want your relationship to work and last.

Conclusion

It's difficult enough for teens and young adults to navigate the complex world of relationships and learn to be independent and responsible along the way. But, when you have autism and are dealing with your own social issues and communication challenges, perhaps while even trying to manage anxiety and depression, being a teen or young adult increases that level of difficulty significantly.

Those are difficult years for sure, and teenagers and young adults with ASD just want what their neuro-typical peers want. Just like others their age, these individuals with ASD want to blend in with their peers, looking and acting like everyone else. They want to find and keep friends and hopefully find boyfriends and girlfriends who they can develop loving relationships with.

Most of them want to get out and do things they enjoy doing with confidence and surety. They don't want to be scared or anxious when they step foot outside their homes. Knowing how to behave and what to expect is just the beginning. Whether they know it or not, they need to understand what kinds of situations they are dealing with and be prepared if things go wrong.

Being independent and respected is important to individuals on the autism spectrum. And although many of them are somewhat naïve and often afraid of taking risks, they still want the chance to prove themselves and to be who they want to be.

I hope that, within this book, especially for those of you on the autism spectrum, you will find useful tips to help make this journey easier and more comfortable. I also hope you will be able to gain the necessary knowledge, confidence and courage to live a fulfilling life.

Resources and Additional Reading

Attwood, S. (2008) *Making Sense of Sex.* (2009) London: Jessica Kingsley Publishers.

Attwood, T., Henault, I., and Dubin, N. (2014) *The Autism Spectrum, Sexuality and the Law: What every parent and professional needs to know.* Jessica Kingsley Publishing.

Attwood, T. (2004) *Exploring Feelings: Cognitive Behaviour Therapy to Manage Anxiety.* Arlington, TX: Future Horizons.

Attwood, T. and Gray, C. (1999) "Understanding and Teaching Friendship Skills." www.tonyattwood.com.au

Cook O'Toole, J. (2013) *The Asper Kids' Secret Book of Social Rules.* Jessica Kingsley Publishers.

Dubin, N. (2009) *Asperger Syndrome and Anxiety: A Guide to Successful Stress Management.* Jessica Kingsley Publishing.

Dubin, N. (2014) *The Autism Spectrum and Depression,* Jessica Kingsley Publishing.

Henault, I. (2006) *Asperger's Syndrome and Sexuality from Adolescence through Adulthood,* London, UK: Jessica Kingsley Publishing.

Hendrickx, S. (2008) *Love, Sex, and Long-Term Relationships: What People with Asperger Syndrome Really Really Want.* London: Jessica Kingsley Publishers.

Hingsburger, D. (1995) *Hand Made Love: A Guide for Teaching About Male Masturbation Through Understanding and Video.* Newmarket: Diverse City Press.

Lawson, W. (2004) *Sex, Sexuality and the Autism Spectrum.* Jessica Kingsley Publishers.

Lipsky, D. and Richards, W. (2009) *Managing Meltdowns: Using the S.C.A.R.E.D Calming Technique with Children and Adults with Autism.* Jessica Kingsley Publishing.

Lipsky, D. (2011) *From Anxiety to Meltdown: How Individuals on the Autism Spectrum Deal with Anxiety, Experience Meltdowns, Manifest Tantrums and How you can Intervene Effectively.* Jessica Kingsley Publishing.

Lohmann, R. C., Taylor, J., Taylor, J.V. (2013) *The Bullying Workbook for Teens: Activities to Help You Deal with Social Aggression and Cyberbullying.* New Harbinger Publications.

Moore, D. and Grandin, T. (2016) *The Loving Push: How Parents and Professionals Can Help Spectrum Kids Become Successful Adults.* Future Horizons, Inc.

Stott, B., and Tickle, A. (2010) *Exploring Bullying with Adults with Autism and Asperger Syndrome: A Photocopiable Workbook.* Jessica Kingsley Publishers.

Wrobel, M. (2003) *Taking Care of Myself-A Hygiene, Puberty and Personal Curriculum for Young People with Autism.* Future Horizons, Inc.

Internet Resources

ActiveBeat.com (2012) "10 Reasons to See Your Dentist", Angela Ayles

Goaskalice.columbia.edu (2005-2016) "Definition of Sex"

Healthline.com (2016) "Balanced Diet", Brian Krans

Lifescript.com (2016) "How to Stay Hydrated", Fran Golden and Monique Ryan

Lifescript.com (2010) "Viral Hepatitis", Debra Wood, RN

Medicaldaily.com(2014) "Sexual Abuse Risk Higher For People with Autism, Prompting Calls for Better Sex Education" Ben Wolford

Nichd.nih.gov (2013) "What are some types of sexually transmitted diseases or sexually transmitted infections?"

Blogs.psychcentral.com (2014) "People on Autism Spectrum at Increased Risk for Substance Abuse" Richard Taite

StressGroup.com "Signs and Symptoms of Depression"

Teachhub.com "Creating Social Stories for Students with Autism and Behavior Disorders"

Un.org "What is Sexual Harassment?"

Vitality.news (2015) "10 Symptoms of Cancer You Are Likely to Ignore" Robert Clive

Waitup.com (2016) "10 Visual Signs You're Actually Not Healthy"

WedMD.com

wikiHow.com "How to Avoid Being Mugged" and "How to Walk Safely at Night"

yourtango.com (2016) "21 Signs You're in an Emotionally Abusive Relationship" Marni Feurman

Also by Mary Wrobel

Taking Care Of Myself

A Healthy Hygiene, Puberty and Personal Curriculum For Young People With Autism

by MARY WROBEL

Puberty can be especially tough when young people have autism or other special needs. Through simple stories similar to Carol Gray's Social Stories, author Mary Wrobel teaches caregivers exactly what to say and not say, and shows how you can create helpful stories of your own. Hygiene, modesty, body growth and development, menstruation, touching, personal safety, and more are addressed. Young students can benefit from self-care skills such as using the toilet, brushing teeth, and washing hands. Parents and teachers should begin teaching these necessary skills as early as possible, even from ages 3-5. The ultimate goal is to maximize the child's potential for independence and lifelong social success

ISBN: 9781885477941

FUTURE HORIZONS INC.

Also available at:

amazon.com

BARNES&NOBLE

BOOKSELLERS

www.bn.com